DR. ALI KESUMA, WPPE.

Fundamentals of Strategic Management

Theory, Practice, and Indonesian Insights

Contents

Preface

This textbook is developed as a comprehensive reference for students, educators, and professionals interested in strategic management within the Indonesian and emerging markets context. It combines foundational theories, practical frameworks, and localized case studies to bridge global knowledge with local relevance.

We hope this book helps readers build strategic thinking that is adaptive, contextual, and impactful.

CHAPTER 1: Introduction to Strategic Management

1.1 Definition and Scope of Strategic Management

Understanding Strategic Management

Strategic management is a series of decisions and actions designed to achieve long-term organizational goals through effective strategy planning, implementation, and evaluation. Strategic management serves as a guide in dealing with changes in a dynamic and competitive business environment.

According to David (2020), strategic management is "the art and science of formulating, implementing, and evaluating cross-functional decisions that enable an organization to achieve its goals."

Rivai & Prawironegoro (2019) explain that strategic management includes various approaches in determining the direction of the company to remain competitive and sustainable in the global market.

Pella (2021) defines strategic management as a systematic process that includes analysis of the internal and external environment, determination of strategic objectives, strategy formulation, implementation, and evaluation to ensure the achievement of organizational goals.

Ramli & Kartini (2022) stated that strategic management is a company's effort to integrate various business functions to increase competitiveness and achieve sustainable growth through environmental analysis, strategy formulation, and effective policy implementation.

Conclusion

Based on the various definitions above, it can be concluded that strategic management is a systematic process that involves planning, implementing, and evaluating organizational strategies to achieve long-term goals. This process includes analysis of the external and internal environment, formulation of adaptive strategies, and management of company resources to maintain competitiveness. With the implementation of effective strategic management, organizations can survive and thrive amidst the ever-changing business dynamics.

Scope of Strategic Management

The scope of strategic management includes three main stages:

1. **Strategy Formulation**

- **External and internal environmental analysis:** Assessing market conditions, competitors, industry trends, and the organization's internal strengths and weaknesses.
- **Identify opportunities and threats:** Determine the factors that can influence the success of the company's strategy.
- **Determining the organization's vision, mission and goals:** Developing long-term goals as a basis for strategic decision making.
- **Business and corporate strategy development:** Developing action plans that will help the organization achieve its goals.

1. **Strategy Implementation**

- **Organizational resource allocation:** Aligning budget, workforce, and technology to support strategy.
- **Strategic policy development:** Establishing guidelines and rules to guide strategy implementation.
- **The role of management in strategy execution:** Coordinating various departments so that the strategy can run effectively.
- **Performance and operational management:** Ensuring that the strategies implemented produce impacts in line with objectives.

1. **Strategy Evaluation and Control**

- **Measuring and evaluating strategy performance:** Monitoring whether the strategy is running according to the established plan.
- **Analysis of the effectiveness of the implemented strategy:** Evaluating the impact of the strategy on the company's growth and competitiveness.
- **Strategy adjustment based on market dynamics:** Changing or adapting strategies according to changes in the business environment.

By understanding the meaning and scope of strategic management, organizations can develop adaptive and innovative strategies to face ever-evolving business challenges.

1.2 The Role of Strategic Management in Organizational Success

The Importance of Strategic Management in Organizations

Strategic management plays a crucial role in the success of an organization, whether on a small or large scale. With the right strategy, an organization can achieve its long-term goals, maintain its competitive advantage, and adapt to changes in the dynamic business environment.

According to David (2020), the success of an organization is highly dependent on its ability to identify opportunities, respond to threats, and allocate resources effectively to achieve the established vision and mission.

Key Role of Strategic Management

Here are some of the main roles of strategic management in organizational success:

1. **Setting the Direction and Goals of the Organization**Strategic management helps organizations determine a clear vision, mission, and long-term goals so that all members of the organization have guidance in carrying out their business activities.
2. **Increasing Competitiveness**By implementing the right strategy, organizations can create a competitive advantage that differentiates them from competitors in the same industry.
3. **Maximizing Resource Utilization**Strategic management enables organizations to allocate resources (financial, human, technological) more effectively to achieve their business goals.
4. **Helping Organizations Adapt to Environmental Change The**ever-changing business environment requires organizations to be flexible and responsive to industry trends, government regulations, and changes in consumer behavior.
5. **Improving Operational Efficiency**A well-crafted strategy can help organizations improve operational efficiency, reduce costs, and increase productivity.
6. **Providing a Basis for Decision Making**By having a clear strategy, management can make more focused decisions based on in-depth analysis of internal and external factors.
7. **Maintaining Business Sustainability**Strategic management ensures that organizations are not only successful in the short term, but can also survive and thrive in the long term through continuous innovation and adaptation.

1.3 History and Development of Strategic Management

Early History of Strategic Management

The concept of strategic management has been around since ancient times, when strategy was used in war and government. This strategic thinking was later adapted in the business world as a way to achieve competitive advantage.

1. **Pre-Modern Era**

- Early strategies were used in a military context, as described by Sun Tzu in *The Art of War* which taught the principles of strategy in dealing with competition.
- Strategic thinking has also developed in government and economics since the era of Ancient Greece and Rome.

1. **Industrial Revolution Era (1750-1900)**

- With the growth of industrialization, there arose the need for planning and organizing on a large scale.
- Frederick Taylor introduced *Scientific Management* which emphasized efficiency and productivity in business operations.

The Development of Strategic Management in the 20th Century

Strategic management began to develop as an academic discipline and structured business practice, especially in the second half of the 20th century.

1. **1950s – The Beginning of the Concept of Strategic Planning**

- Alfred Chandler (1962) stated that the organizational structure must follow the strategy set by the company.
- The concept of strategic planning is starting to be applied in large

companies to accommodate business growth.

1. **1960s – The Emergence of Environmental and Competitive Analysis**

- Igor Ansoff introduced *Corporate Strategy* , which emphasized the importance of environmental analysis in formulating strategy.
- The concept of *SWOT Analysis* was introduced as a method of evaluating internal and external factors of an organization.

1. **1970s – Porter's Five Forces Model**

- Michael Porter developed the *Five Forces model* that helps companies analyze industry competitiveness.
- Strategic management is increasingly oriented towards competitive advantage and generic strategies such as differentiation and cost leadership.

1. **1980s – Focus on Strategy Implementation**

- There is a growing awareness that strategies must not only be formulated but also implemented effectively.
- *Balanced Scorecard* concept was developed to measure strategy performance more comprehensively.

1. **1990s – The Era of Globalization and Technology**

- Information technology and globalization accelerate business change and require companies to have flexible and innovative strategies.
- *Core Competencies* concept underlines the importance of a company's core competencies in building a sustainable business strategy.

Strategic Management in the Digital and Disruption Era

Entering the 21st century, strategic management is undergoing a major transformation with the emergence of digital technology, artificial intelligence, and disruptive business models.

1. **2000s – Digitalization and Strategic Innovation**

- Companies are starting to leverage digital technologies to create data-driven and artificial intelligence-driven strategies.
- *Platform economy* business models such as those implemented by Amazon, Google, and Uber are disrupting traditional industries.

1. **2010s – Agile Strategy and Rapid Adaptation**

- *Agile Strategy* approach is beginning to be adopted, allowing companies to be more flexible in responding to market changes.
- *Sustainability* strategies are becoming increasingly important with increasing awareness of social and environmental responsibility.

1. **2020s – Strategy Management in the Age of AI and Big Data**

- AI technology and *big data analytics* are changing the way organizations develop business strategies.
- The focus on *resilience strategy* is gaining more attention, especially after the global pandemic which taught us the importance of a resilient strategy in the face of uncertainty.

Conclusion

The history and development of strategic management shows that strategic approaches continue to evolve in line with changes in the business environment. From military strategies to AI-based strategies, companies must continue to adapt to stay relevant and competitive in the global marketplace. Understanding these developments allows organizations to be more adaptive and innovative in facing future business challenges.

1.4 Benefits of Strategic Management for Companies

Strategic management provides various benefits for companies in facing increasingly tight business competition. Effective strategy implementation allows companies to achieve their long-term goals and adapt to changes in the business environment. Here are some of the main benefits of strategic management for companies:

1. Provide Clear Direction and Focus

Strategic management helps companies formulate clear visions, missions, and long-term goals. With a structured strategy, every part of the organization has a guide to carry out tasks and make decisions that are in line with the company's goals.

2. Increase Competitive Advantage

Through analysis of the external and internal environment, strategic management enables companies to identify competitive advantages that can be utilized to win the competition in the industry. The right strategy helps companies create added value for customers and strengthen their market position.

3. Facilitates Adaptation to Changes in the Business Environment

The business environment is constantly changing due to technological developments, regulatory changes, and global economic dynamics. With a strategic approach, companies can respond quickly to changes and adjust their business strategies to stay relevant and competitive.

4. Optimizing Resource Utilization

A well-designed strategy enables companies to allocate resources (financial, human, and technological) more efficiently. Optimal resource management helps companies avoid waste and increase productivity.

5. Improve Coordination and Synergy within the Organization

Strategic management ensures that all business units are working in the same direction to achieve common goals. With an integrated strategy, companies can improve coordination between departments and create stronger synergies.

6. Improve Decision Making Ability

The strategic management process provides a solid foundation for data-driven and analytical decision-making. With a clear strategy, managers can make more rational, fact-based, and market-appropriate decisions.

7. Reducing Risk and Uncertainty

Strategic management allows companies to identify potential risks that can affect business performance. With careful planning, companies can anticipate and manage risks better, thereby reducing the negative impact on company operations.

8. Improve Company Performance and Profitability

An effective strategy can improve operational efficiency and overall business effectiveness. By implementing the right strategy, companies can achieve sustainable growth, increase revenue, and improve profitability.

9. Increase Resilience in Crisis

In a crisis situation such as a pandemic or economic recession, companies with a strong strategy are better able to survive and recover compared to companies without good planning. Strategic management allows companies to have contingency plans in the face of uncertainty.

10. Increase Company Value for Stakeholders

Companies that are managed with good strategies tend to be more attractive to investors, business partners, and customers. With a strategy that is oriented towards long-term growth, companies can increase stakeholder trust and create greater value.

Conclusion

Strategic management is a very important tool for companies to run their business effectively and sustainably. With the right strategy, companies can have a clear direction, stronger competitiveness, and the ability to face business challenges better. Implementing good strategic management not only improves performance and profits, but also ensures that companies remain relevant in a dynamic market.

Case Study: Strategy Analysis in Indonesian Companies

Background

PT XYZ is a manufacturing company engaged in the textile industry in Indonesia. The company has been operating for more than 20 years and has various products sold in both domestic and export markets. However, in the last five years, PT XYZ has faced various challenges, such as increasing competition from imported products, changing consumer trends, and fluctuations in raw material prices. To remain competitive, the company's management has begun implementing new business strategies that include digitalization, product diversification, and supply chain optimization.

The problem

Despite implementing a new strategy, PT XYZ still faces several obstacles, including:

1. Difficulty in adapting strategies to rapidly changing business environments.
2. Increasingly tight price competition from imported products with lower production costs.
3. Limited resources in implementing digitalization comprehensively.
4. Lack of understanding among employees about the importance of the new strategies being implemented.

Student Assignment

As a business strategy analyst, you are asked to help PT XYZ in developing a more effective strategy by answering the following questions:

1. **Environmental Analysis**

- Identify the external environmental factors (Opportunities and Threats) and internal factors (Strengths and Weaknesses) faced by PT XYZ.

- Use SWOT analysis to analyze the company's condition.

1. **Strategy Formulation**

- Based on the SWOT analysis that has been conducted, recommend strategies that can help PT XYZ increase its competitiveness.
- Is the product diversification strategy carried out by PT XYZ appropriate? Give your justification.

1. **Strategy Implementation**

- How can PT XYZ overcome obstacles in implementing digitalization?
- What steps should be taken to improve employee understanding of the new strategies implemented?

1. **Strategy Evaluation**

- How to measure the effectiveness of the strategies implemented by PT XYZ?
- Provide suggestions regarding strategy evaluation and control so that PT XYZ remains competitive in the textile industry.

Expected Output:

- A strategic analysis report that includes a SWOT analysis, strategic recommendations, implementation steps, and evaluation methods.
- A short presentation on strategies that can be implemented by PT XYZ.

CHAPTER 2: Vision, Mission, and Objectives of the Organization

2.1 Definition of Vision and Mission

Understanding Vision

Vision is a statement that describes the long-term goals of an organization and the direction it wants to achieve in the future. Vision provides inspiration and a picture of the future desired by the organization.

According to David (2020), a vision is "a clear image of the future desired by a company, which serves as a guide in strategic decision making."

Rivai & Prawironegoro (2019) explain that an organization's vision is "a guide that helps a company determine its long-term direction and ensures that all elements in the organization work towards the same goal."

Pella (2021) added that the vision must be ambitious, but still realistic and achievable by the organization within a certain period.

Ramli & Kartini (2022) stated that the vision must be able to inspire and motivate all elements in the organization to continue to develop and innovate.

Definition of Mission

A mission is a statement that explains the reason for an organization's existence, the main goals it wants to achieve, and how the organization operates to achieve its stated vision.

According to David (2020), a mission is "a statement that defines the fundamental aims and objectives of an organization, as well as how the organization creates value for its stakeholders."

Rivai & Prawironegoro (2019) stated that the mission reflects the identity of the organization and the role it plays in its business environment.

Pella (2021) added that the mission must be clear, specific, and can be used as a basis for making operational decisions.

Ramli & Kartini (2022) argue that the mission must be able to describe the core values of the organization and provide more specific direction for daily operations.

Difference between Vision and Mission

Conclusion

Vision and mission are important elements in strategic management because they form the basis for formulating and implementing organizational strategies. Vision provides a big picture of long-term goals, while mission explains how the organization will achieve those goals through real actions.

2.2 Elements of an Effective Vision and Mission

Elements of an Effective Vision

A good vision must meet several important elements in order to be a clear guideline for the organization in the long term. According to David (2020), an effective vision has the following elements:

1. **Future Oriented**

- The vision should describe the ideal condition that the organization wants to achieve in the next few years.

1. **Contains Company Values and Philosophy**

- Must reflect the core values and culture of the organization that will guide decision making.

1. **Inspirational and Motivating**

- The vision must be able to inspire members of the organization and related parties to contribute to achieving it.

1. **Realistic and Achievable**

- While ambitious, the vision must remain within the bounds of what is possible to realize.

1. **Short and Clear**

- The vision statement must be easily understood by all elements of the organization.

1. **Flexible and Adaptive**

- The vision must be flexible enough to adapt to changes in the business environment and technology.

Elements of an Effective Mission

An effective mission must be able to describe the main objectives of the organization and how to achieve them. According to Rivai & Prawironegoro (2019), the main elements in compiling an effective mission include:

1. **Organizational Objectives**

- Explains why the organization was founded and the goals it wants to achieve.

1. **Products and Services**

- Identify the major products or services the organization offers to the market.

1. **Markets and Customers Served**

- Determine the market segments and target customers that the organization wants to reach.

1. **Competitive Advantage**

- Explains what differentiates the organization from competitors and how the company creates unique value.

1. **Organizational Values and Culture**

- The mission should reflect the principles and values that the organization holds dear.

1. **Social Responsibility**

- Expresses the organization's commitment to broader social and environmental interests.

1. **Goal Achievement Strategy**

- Describes how the organization operates to achieve its vision and mission.

Examples of Company Vision and Mission in Indonesia

Here are some examples of visions and missions of large companies in Indonesia:

1. **PT Bank Rakyat Indonesia (BRI)Vision:** "To Become The Most Valuable Banking Group in Southeast Asia & Champion of Financial Inclusion." **Mission:**

- Providing excellent and sustainable banking services.
- Expanding financial access for all levels of society.
- Driving economic growth through support for MSMEs.

1. **PT Telkom IndonesiaVision:** "To become the Digital Telco of choice to advance society." **Mission:**

- Providing the best and innovative digital services.
- Developing a sustainable digital ecosystem.
- Enhancing global competitiveness through technology.

1. **PT Unilever IndonesiaVision:** "To be a company that makes life better

through innovative and sustainable products." **Mission:**

- Providing quality products that are beneficial to society.
- Reducing environmental impact through responsible operations.
- Creating value for shareholders and other stakeholders.

1. **PT Astra International TbkVision:** "Prosperity together with the nation." **Mission:**

- Running a sustainable business with good governance.
- Making a positive contribution to society and the environment.
- Improving employee and stakeholder welfare.

1. **PT Pertamina (Persero)Vision:** "To become a world-class national energy company." **Mission:**

- Providing quality energy for all Indonesian people.
- Developing innovation in the energy and petrochemical industry.
- Running a business with the principles of sustainability and good governance.

Conclusion

An effective vision and mission are critical to an organization's success. A strong vision provides a picture of the organization's long-term goals, while a clear mission ensures that every action taken is aligned with the business's values and strategy. Organizations with an effective vision and mission are better able to meet business challenges and achieve competitive advantage.

2.3 Relationship between Vision, Mission, and Organizational Goals

The Relationship between Vision, Mission, and Organizational Goals

The vision, mission, and goals of an organization are closely related in shaping the company's strategy and direction. These three elements work synergistically to ensure that every action taken by the organization is in line with its long-term strategy.

1. **Vision as the Main Guide**

- Vision sets out the big picture of the future that the organization wants to achieve.
- Vision provides inspiration and motivation to all stakeholders.
- As a basis for formulating the organization's mission and objectives.

1. **Mission as Implementation of Vision**

- The mission defines how the organization will achieve its stated vision.
- Describes the role of the organization, the services or products offered, and the values it upholds.
- Connecting the vision with real actions taken by the company.

1. **Goals as Real Steps**

- Organizational objectives are specific statements that describe the results to be achieved within a certain period.
- It is more measurable and can be translated into operational strategies and plans.
- To be an evaluation tool to assess whether the vision and mission have been achieved effectively.

The Structure of the Relationship between Vision, Mission, and Organizational Goals

The relationship between vision, mission and goals can be described in the following structure:

- **Vision** → Determines the main direction of the organization in the long term.
- **Mission** → Describes the strategic steps to realize the vision.
- **Objectives** → Are concrete achievements that are used as a benchmark for the success of mission implementation.

For example, if a company has a vision of "To be a leader in the green technology industry," then:

- The mission could be "To develop innovative products based on high quality and environmentally friendly renewable energy."
- The objectives that can be implemented include:
- Increase the market share of environmentally friendly products by 20% in 3 years.
- Developing energy-saving technology with 30% higher efficiency than previous products.
- Establish partnerships with 10 companies providing environmentally friendly raw materials.

The SMART Approach to Goal Setting

In order for organizational goals to be more effective, you can use the **SMART approach** , which stands for:

1. **Specific (Specific):**

- The objectives must be clear and specific so as not to give rise to different interpretations.

- Example: "Increase green product sales by 20% within 2 years."

1. **Measurable:**

- Goals must have measurable indicators to assess progress.
- Example: "Adding 1,000 new customers in one year."

1. **Achievable (Can be achieved):**

- Goals must be realistic and achievable based on the organization's capacity and resources.
- Example: "Reduce production waste by 15% in one year with new technology."

1. **Relevant:**

- Objectives must be in line with the organization's vision and mission and have a positive impact on the company.
- Example: "Improve energy efficiency to support the company's sustainability strategy."

1. **Time-Bound:**

- Goals must have a clear time limit to achieve.
- Example: "Develop three innovative products in the eco-friendly category within 18 months."

By applying the SMART principle, organizations can ensure that each goal set not only supports the vision and mission, but can also be evaluated objectively.

Conclusion

The vision, mission, and objectives of an organization have complementary roles in shaping business strategy. Vision becomes a long-term direction, mission provides a framework for how the vision can be realized, while objectives set specific targets that can be measured to assess the success of implementing the organization's strategy. By using the **SMART approach**, organizational objectives can be designed more effectively and provide a more real impact in implementing business strategy.

2.4 Examples of Vision and Mission of Successful Companies

A strong and clear vision and mission are essential for a company's success. Here are some examples of visions and missions from successful companies in Indonesia that can be used as references:

1. PT Bank Rakyat Indonesia (BRI)

Vision: "To become the Most Valuable Banking Group in Southeast Asia & Champion of Financial Inclusion."
Mission:

- Providing excellent and sustainable banking services.
- Expanding financial access for all levels of society.
- Driving economic growth through support for MSMEs.

2. PT Telkom Indonesia

Vision: "To become the Digital Telco of choice to advance society."
Mission:

- Providing the best and innovative digital services.

- Developing a sustainable digital ecosystem.
- Enhancing global competitiveness through technology.

3. PT Unilever Indonesia

Vision: "To be a company that makes life better through innovative and sustainable products."
Mission:

- Providing quality products that are beneficial to society.
- Reducing environmental impact through responsible operations.
- Creating value for shareholders and other stakeholders.

4. PT Astra International Tbk

Vision: "Prosperity together with the nation."
Mission:

- Running a sustainable business with good governance.
- Making a positive contribution to society and the environment.
- Improving employee and stakeholder welfare.

5. PT Pertamina (Persero)

Vision: "To become a world-class national energy company."
Mission:

- Providing quality energy for all Indonesian people.
- Developing innovation in the energy and petrochemical industry.

- Running a business with the principles of sustainability and good governance.

Conclusion

From the examples above, it can be seen that successful companies have a clear vision and mission that are aligned with their business strategy. The vision provides long-term direction, while the mission explains how the company achieves those goals. Companies with a strong vision and mission tend to be better able to adapt to change, increase competitiveness, and provide added value to their stakeholders.

Case Study: Comparison of Company Vision and Mission in Indonesia

Background

Vision and mission are the main foundations in strategic management of an organization. Each company has a different vision and mission, which are adjusted to the business objectives, company values, and business environment faced. A company with a strong vision and mission tends to have a clearer direction in strategic decision making.

Two large companies in Indonesia, **PT Bank Rakyat Indonesia (BRI)** and **PT Telkom Indonesia** , have visions and missions that reflect their business focus. This case study will compare how the two companies implement their visions and missions in their daily business practices.

Company Description

1. **PT Bank Rakyat Indonesia (BRI)**

- **Vision:** "To become the Most Valuable Banking Group in Southeast Asia

& Champion of Financial Inclusion."
- **Mission:**
- Providing excellent and sustainable banking services.
- Expanding financial access for all levels of society.
- Driving economic growth through support for MSMEs.

1. **PT Telkom Indonesia**

- **Vision:** "To become the Digital Telco of choice to advance society."
- **Mission:**
- Providing the best and innovative digital services.
- Developing a sustainable digital ecosystem.
- Enhancing global competitiveness through technology.

Case Study Analysis

1. **Vision Comparison**

- BRI focuses more on inclusive financial services that can reach all levels of society, especially MSMEs.
- Telkom Indonesia is more oriented towards digital transformation and technological innovation for the advancement of society.

1. **Mission Comparison**

- BRI has a mission that places greater emphasis on the role of banks in providing sustainable and inclusive financial services.
- Telkom Indonesia focuses on developing digital services and technological innovations that can increase global competitiveness.

1. **Implementation in Business Strategy**

- **BRI** : Running various financial inclusion programs such as People's Business Credit (KUR), digitalization of banking services, and CSR programs for community economic empowerment.

- **Telkom Indonesia** : Developing high-quality internet networks, cloud computing services, and digital acceleration programs for MSMEs and start-ups.

Student Assignment

As a business strategy analyst, you are asked to compare the vision and mission of two other Indonesian companies of your own choosing. Answer the following questions in the strategy analysis report:

1. Choose two Indonesian companies from different industrial sectors, then write down their vision and mission.
2. Analyze the suitability of the company's vision and mission with their business model.
3. Evaluate the implementation of each company's business strategy based on their vision and mission.
4. Provide recommendations on how companies can better align their vision and mission with the business challenges they face.

Expected Output:

- Strategy analysis report minimum **3 pages** .
- A short presentation on the results of a comparative analysis of the vision and mission of the two companies.

CHAPTER 3: External Environmental Analysis

3.1 Concept of Macro and Micro External Environment

Definition of External Environment

The external environment includes all factors outside the organization that can affect the company's business operations and strategies. These external factors are dynamic and often beyond the company's control, but must still be analyzed to formulate effective strategies.

According to David (2020), the external environment is "conditions and trends outside the organization that can create opportunities or threats to the business." Rivai & Prawironegoro (2019) added that understanding the external environment is very important to increase the company's competitiveness in facing market changes.

The external environment falls into two main categories:

1. Macro External Environment

The macro environment includes factors that affect the industry at large and are usually beyond the direct control of the company. Some of the major factors in the macro environment include:

- **Economic Factors**
- **Inflation:** Moderate inflation can drive economic growth because it increases people's purchasing power. However, high inflation can increase production costs and reduce customers' purchasing power, thus harming companies.
- **Interest Rates:** Low interest rates make it easier for businesses and consumers to access credit, boosting business growth. However, high interest rates can increase borrowing costs and hinder business expansion.
- **Currency Exchange Rates:** A stable currency helps international trade, while exchange rate fluctuations can increase financial risks for companies that rely on imports or exports.
- **Political and Regulatory Factors**
- **Government Policy:** Regulations that favor certain industries can create opportunities for companies, while strict regulations can be a hindrance.
- **Political Stability:** A stable political environment supports investment, while political uncertainty can hamper business growth.
- **Social and Demographic Factors**
- **Consumption Trends:** Changing lifestyles and consumer preferences create opportunities for product innovation.
- **Population Growth:** High population growth expands the potential market, but can also increase competition for labor.
- **Technology Factors**
- **Technological Innovation:** New technologies improve production efficiency and provide competitive advantage.
- **Digital Disruption:** Companies that do not adapt to digital technologies risk being left behind by the competition.
- **Environmental Factors**
- **Climate Change:** Strict environmental regulations can increase operational costs, but businesses that practice sustainability can gain a positive image.
- **Sustainability:** Consumers are increasingly concerned about environmentally friendly products, creating opportunities for green business-oriented companies.

- **Legal Factors**
- **Labor Regulation:** Strong labor protections can improve employee well-being, but can increase operating costs.
- **Intellectual Property Rights:** Patent and trademark protection provides an advantage to companies that innovate.

2. Micro External Environment

The microenvironment is closer to the company's operations and consists of elements that have a direct impact on the business. Some of the key factors in the microenvironment include:

- **Competitors**
- **Healthy Competition:** Encouraging innovation and improving product quality.
- **Unhealthy Competition:** Price wars can reduce a company's profitability.
- **Customer**
- **Customer Loyalty:** Provides stable income for the company.
- **Changing Preferences:** Forcing companies to continuously innovate to stay relevant.
- **Suppliers**
- **Reliable Supplier:** Ensure the stability of raw material supply.
- **Dependence on Certain Suppliers:** Can increase risk if there is a disruption in the supply chain.
- **Distributors and Business Partners**
- **Efficient Distribution:** Accelerate product delivery to the market.
- **Logistics Constraints:** Can hinder the smooth running of company operations.
- **Stakeholders**
- **Supporting Investors:** Providing capital for business expansion.
- **Social Demand:** Pressure from society to implement responsible business

policies.

Conclusion

The external environment has a significant impact on a company's business strategy. A deep understanding of macro and micro factors allows companies to identify opportunities and anticipate threats. Therefore, companies must continue to analyze the external environment to ensure a flexible and adaptive strategy to market changes.

3.2 PESTEL Model in Analyzing the External Environment

Understanding the PESTEL Model

PESTEL model is an analytical tool used to evaluate external factors that can affect an organization's performance and strategy. PESTEL stands for **Political, Economic, Social, Technological, Environmental, and Legal** . This analysis helps organizations understand the challenges and opportunities that exist in their business environment.

According to David (2020), PESTEL analysis helps companies identify external trends that can impact business strategies. Rivai & Prawironegoro (2019) added that a deep understanding of PESTEL factors allows companies to anticipate changes and develop more adaptive strategies.

Factors in the PESTEL Model

1. **Political (Politics)**

- **Definition:** Political factors include government policies, political stability, industry regulations, tax rates, and international trade relations.

- **Positive Impact:** Regulations that support certain industries can open up new market opportunities and increase competitiveness.
- **Negative Impact:** Political instability and sudden policy changes can create business uncertainty.
- **Example:** The Indonesian government supports the electric vehicle industry with various tax incentives, which provides opportunities for companies such as Hyundai and Wuling to invest in Indonesia.

1. Economic (Economy)

- **Definition:** Economic factors include inflation, interest rates, exchange rates, economic growth, and unemployment rates.
- **Positive Impact:** Strong economic growth increases consumer purchasing power and business expansion opportunities.
- **Negative Impact:** High inflation can increase production costs and reduce customer purchasing power.
- **Example:** The COVID-19 pandemic caused a global economic slowdown, but also encouraged the growth of e-commerce such as Tokopedia and Shopee which experienced an increase in online transactions.

1. Social (Social)

- **Definition:** Social factors include culture, lifestyle, demographic trends, education levels, and changes in customer behavior.
- **Positive Impact:** Lifestyle changes can open up new market opportunities for certain industries.
- **Negative Impact:** Rapid social change can cause products or services to become obsolete.
- **Example:** The healthy lifestyle trend in Indonesia is increasing the demand for organic products and health services such as those developed by health startup Halodoc.

1. **Technological (Technology)**

- **Definition:** Technological factors include technological innovation, digitalization, automation, and the development of artificial intelligence (AI).
- **Positive Impact:** New technologies can improve operational efficiency and create competitive advantages.
- **Negative Impact:** Companies that fail to adopt new technologies risk losing competitiveness.
- **Example:** Gojek integrates AI into its booking and route optimization system to improve customer experience and operational efficiency.

1. **Environmental (Environment)**

- **Definition:** Environmental factors include climate change, environmental regulation, sustainability, and natural resource use.
- **Positive Impact:** Companies that implement sustainable business practices can improve their brand image and attract environmentally conscious customers.
- **Negative Impact:** Strict environmental regulations can increase operating costs.
- **Example:** Companies like Danone-AQUA implement sustainability strategies with plastic bottle recycling programs to reduce environmental impact.

1. **Legal (Law)**

- **Definition:** Legal factors include employment regulations, consumer protection, business regulations, and intellectual property rights.
- **Positive Impact:** Clear and stable laws can provide legal certainty for companies.
- **Negative Impact:** Sudden regulatory changes can increase compliance costs.

- **Example:** The Personal Data Protection Act in Indonesia encourages technology companies such as Bukalapak and Tokopedia to improve user data security.

Real Examples of Implementing PESTEL Analysis in Indonesian Companies

For example, the following is the application of PESTEL analysis at **PT Gojek Indonesia** , a technology company based on transportation applications and digital services.

1. **Political:** Online transportation regulations implemented by the Indonesian government set upper and lower tariff limits, providing legal certainty for Gojek but also limiting price flexibility.
2. **Economic:** The growth of the digital economy encourages the use of application-based services, such as GoPay and GoFood. However, high inflation can reduce customer purchasing power.
3. **Social:** Digital consumption trends and fast-paced lifestyles increase demand for Gojek services, especially during the pandemic when physical mobility is limited.
4. **Technological:** Gojek leverages AI and big data to improve customer experience and optimize driver routes.
5. **Environmental:** Gojek has started investing in electric vehicles to reduce its carbon footprint.
6. **Legal:** Digital tax regulations and personal data protection provisions require Gojek to ensure compliance with applicable laws.

Conclusion

The PESTEL model is a very useful analytical tool in understanding the external factors that affect a business. By conducting an in-depth analysis of **political, economic, social, technological, environmental and legal factors** , companies can develop more effective strategies and increase their competitiveness in the market.

3.3 Porter's Five Forces Analysis

Understanding Porter's Five Forces Model

Porter's Five Forces Model was developed by Michael E. Porter as an analytical tool to understand the dynamics of competition in an industry. This model helps companies evaluate the level of competition and identify external factors that can affect profitability and business strategy.

According to Porter (1980), the five forces that shape industrial competitiveness are:

1. **Threat of New Entrants**
2. **Supplier Bargaining Power**
3. **Buyer Bargaining Power**
4. **Threat of Substitute Products or Services**
5. **Competition between Companies in the Industry**

By understanding these factors, companies can design more effective strategies to face competition in the market.

Porter's Five Forces and Their Impact on Business Strategy

1. **Threat of New Entrants**

- **Definition:** The ease or barriers for new firms to enter a particular industry.
- **Influencing Factors:** Economies of scale, capital requirements, regulation, brand loyalty, and access to distribution.
- **Positive Impact:** If entry barriers are high, existing firms have a competitive advantage.
- **Negative Impact:** If entry barriers are low, the industry will be more competitive with the entry of new players.
- **Example:** The telecommunications industry has high barriers to entry because it requires large infrastructure investments.

1. **Supplier Bargaining Power**

- **Definition:** How much suppliers can influence the price and availability of raw materials.
- **Influencing Factors:** Number of suppliers, product differentiation, and the importance of suppliers to the industry.
- **Positive Impact:** If the bargaining power of suppliers is low, the company has flexibility in price negotiations.
- **Negative Impact:** If suppliers have high bargaining power, they can raise the prices of raw materials, which increases production costs.
- **Example:** The automotive industry relies on parts suppliers, who can determine the price and availability of materials.

1. **Buyer Bargaining Power**

- **Definition:** How much customers can influence the price and quality of a product.
- **Influencing Factors:** Number of customers, product differentiation, and

availability of alternatives.

- **Positive Impact:** If customer bargaining power is low, companies can set higher prices and maintain profit margins.
- **Negative Impact:** If customers have high bargaining power, they can press down prices and demand higher quality.
- **Example:** In the retail industry, customers have many choices, so they can demand more competitive prices.

1. **Threat of Substitute Products or Services**

- **Definition:** The risk that other products may replace the primary product in a particular industry.
- **Influencing Factors:** Price and performance of substitute products, customer loyalty, and switching costs.
- **Positive Impact:** If substitute products have low competitiveness, the industry remains stable.
- **Negative Impact:** If substitute products are cheaper or superior, companies must innovate to remain competitive.
- **Example:** The transportation industry faces threats from ride-sharing services such as Gojek and Grab which are replacing conventional taxis.

1. **Competition between Companies in the Industry**

- **Definition:** The level of competition between companies in the same industry.
- **Influencing Factors:** Number of competitors, market growth, product differentiation, and fixed costs.
- **Positive Impact:** If competition is low, companies can enjoy higher profit margins.
- **Negative Impact:** If competition is high, companies must continue to innovate and increase efficiency to survive.

- **Example:** The smartphone industry has high competition with brands like Samsung, Apple, and Xiaomi continuing to innovate.

Application of Porter's Five Forces Analysis in Business Strategy

This analysis helps companies to:

- Identify the main factors that influence competitiveness in the industry.
- Adjusting business strategies to address threats and take advantage of opportunities.
- Determining whether an industry is worth entering or developing further.
- Designing more effective differentiation, cost leadership, or market focus strategies.

For example, **PT Indofood Sukses Makmur Tbk** implements a product diversification and distribution strengthening strategy to face high competition in the food and beverage industry.

Conclusion

Porter's Five Forces model provides a deep understanding of the competitive dynamics in a particular industry. By conducting a thorough analysis of **the threat of new entrants, supplier bargaining power, buyer bargaining power, threat of substitute products, and rivalry among firms** , companies can develop more effective strategies to survive and thrive in the market.

3.4 Implications of the External Environment on Strategy

Understanding the Implications of the External Environment on Strategy

The external environment has a significant influence on the formulation and implementation of organizational strategies. Companies must be able to adapt their strategies based on changes in the external environment in order to remain competitive and sustainable.

According to David (2020), changes in political, economic, social, technological, environmental, and legal factors can create opportunities or threats for organizations. Therefore, companies must continue to analyze the external environment and adjust their strategies flexibly.

How External Environment Affects Business Strategy

1. **Political and Regulatory Factors**

- **Impact on strategy:** Changes in government policies, tax regulations, and trade policies can affect a company's operations.
- **Example strategy:** Companies can lobby for policies or adopt business models that comply with the latest regulations. For example, the fintech industry adjusts their services to the Financial Services Authority (OJK) regulations.

1. **Economic Factors**

- **Impact on strategy:** Fluctuations in exchange rates, inflation and interest rates affect operating costs and consumer purchasing power.
- **Example strategy:** Companies can implement cost efficiency or revenue diversification strategies to reduce dependence on certain markets.

1. **Social and Demographic Factors**

- **Impact on strategy:** Changes in consumer behavior and market preferences can create new business opportunities.
- **Strategy example:** Companies can adapt marketing strategies to suit social trends, such as the increasing demand for organic and sustainable products.

1. **Technology Factors**

- **Impact on strategy:** Rapid technological developments can change existing business models.
- **Example strategy:** Companies can invest in digitalization, artificial intelligence, and data analytics to increase efficiency and competitiveness.

1. **Environmental Factors**

- **Impact on strategy:** Environmental regulations and social pressures on sustainability can impact business operations.
- **Example strategy:** Companies can develop green policies, such as the use of renewable energy and recycling programs.

1. **Legal Factors**

- **Impact on strategy:** Changes in employment and consumer protection laws may impact a company's operational policies.
- **Strategy example:** Companies can improve legal compliance and ensure that their business policies are aligned with applicable regulations.

Case Study: Implications of External Environment on Indonesian Companies

For example, **PT Unilever Indonesia** adjusted their strategy to face external environmental challenges:

- **Economic Factors:** With the increasing price of raw materials, Unilever implemented operational efficiency strategies to reduce production costs.
- **Social Factors:** Changes in consumer preferences towards environmentally friendly products have led Unilever to develop products based on natural ingredients and environmentally friendly packaging.
- **Technology Factors:** Unilever is investing in digital marketing and e-commerce to increase customer engagement and market penetration.
- **Environmental Factors:** Government regulations regarding plastic waste reduction have encouraged Unilever to adopt a strategy of recycling and reducing plastic in its packaging.

Conclusion

The external environment has a major impact on a company's strategy. By conducting a proper analysis of external factors, companies can adjust their business strategies to meet challenges and take advantage of opportunities. The success of an organization depends largely on its flexibility and ability to adapt to environmental changes.

Case Study: The Impact of External Environment on Indonesian Companies

Background

PT XYZ is an electronics manufacturing company based in Indonesia. Over the past decade, the company has grown rapidly in the local market and has begun targeting expansion into the Southeast Asian market. However, in recent years, PT XYZ has faced challenges from changes in the external environment, including exchange rate fluctuations, government policies related to the electronics industry, digitalization trends, and changing consumer preferences for environmentally friendly products.

PT XYZ management realizes that to remain competitive, they need to analyze external factors that affect their business and adjust the company's strategy to be more adaptive to these changes.

The problem

Currently, PT XYZ is facing several major challenges:

1. **Political and Regulatory Factors:** The government has imposed new regulations requiring the use of local components in electronic products.
2. **Economic Factors:** Fluctuations in the Rupiah exchange rate against the US Dollar increase the cost of importing raw materials.
3. **Social Factors:** Consumers are increasingly aware of environmentally friendly products, while PT XYZ still uses old technology that is less energy efficient.
4. **Technology Factors:** Advances in artificial intelligence and IoT (Internet of Things) open up opportunities for product innovation, but PT XYZ is still lagging behind in implementing these technologies.
5. **Environmental Factors:** Strict regulations regarding e-waste force PT XYZ to invest in better waste management.
6. **Legal Factors:** Consumer protection laws are increasingly being tightened, so PT XYZ must improve the quality of its after-sales service.

Student Assignment

As a business strategy consultant, you are asked to help PT XYZ in developing a more effective strategy by answering the following questions:

1. **PESTEL Analysis**

- Identify opportunities and threats for PT XYZ based on PESTEL factors.
- How can companies optimize opportunities and mitigate threats from the external environment?

1. **Porter's Five Forces Analysis**

- Competitive analysis in the electronics industry using Porter's Five Forces model.
- How can PT XYZ improve its competitiveness by considering the threat of new entrants, the bargaining power of suppliers and customers, and competition in the industry?

1. **Implementable Business Strategies**

- Recommend strategies that PT XYZ can use to deal with changes in the external environment.
- How can companies leverage technology and sustainability trends to improve competitiveness?

1. **Strategy Evaluation and Implementation**

- How does PT XYZ evaluate the effectiveness of the strategies implemented?
- What indicators of success can be used to assess the impact of the strategies that have been implemented?

Expected Output:

- Strategy analysis report covering PESTEL analysis and Porter's Five Forces.
- Recommended business strategies that can be implemented by PT XYZ.
- A short presentation on solutions that can be implemented by PT XYZ.

CHAPTER 4: Internal Environmental Analysis

4.1 Concept of Resources and Capabilities

Understanding Resources and Capabilities

Resources and capabilities are important elements in the analysis of a company's internal environment. Resources refer to the assets owned by the company, both tangible and intangible, while capabilities reflect the organization's ability to combine and utilize these resources to achieve competitive advantage.

According to Barney (1991), company resources can be categorized as:

1. **Tangible Resources:** Includes physical assets such as equipment, infrastructure, and financial capital.
2. **Intangible Resources:** Including brand reputation, patents, technology, and organizational culture.
3. **Human Resources:** The skills, experience, and competencies of employees in supporting organizational excellence.

Firm capabilities relate to how an organization effectively uses resources to create value. These capabilities include innovation, operational efficiency, marketing capabilities, and managerial skills.

The Importance of Resources and Capabilities in Business Strategy

The resources and capabilities owned by the company play an important role in building a sustainable business strategy:

1. **Creating Competitive Advantage:** Companies with unique and difficult-to-imitate resources can gain a strong competitive position.
2. **Determining Product Differentiation:** Innovation and operational capabilities enable a company to offer unique products or services.
3. **Improving Operational Efficiency:** Well-managed resources can reduce costs and increase productivity.
4. **Accelerating Growth and Expansion:** Strong financial resources and managerial capabilities enable the company to expand into new markets.

The Role of Resources in Internal Environmental Analysis

Each type of company resource plays an important role in the analysis of the internal environment. Here is the impact of various resources on business strategy:

1. **Tangible Resources**

- **Physical Assets:** If a company has modern and sufficient physical assets, this can support competitive advantage. Conversely, limited or outdated assets can be a barrier to operations and innovation.
- **Financial Capital:** Companies with strong financial capital are more flexible in making strategic investments. However, financial constraints can hamper growth and competitiveness.

1. **Intangible Resources**

- **Brand Reputation:** Companies with a good reputation have an advantage in attracting customers and maintaining market loyalty. However, a bad

image or scandal can damage a company's competitive position.
- **Patents and Technology:** Companies that have proprietary technology can dominate the market, while a lack of innovation can leave a company behind competitors.

1. **Human Resources**

- **Employee Competence:** Skilled and experienced employees can increase a company's productivity and innovation. However, limited workforce skills can be a significant weakness.
- **Organizational Culture:** A work culture that supports collaboration and innovation will accelerate the growth of the company. Conversely, a poor work culture can hinder the effectiveness of the organization.

Conclusion

Resource and capability analysis is essential in business strategy. Companies that understand the strengths and weaknesses of their resources can design strategies that are more effective and adaptive to changes in the business environment. The role of each type of resource must be considered in the analysis of the internal environment so that the company can determine the strategy that best suits the conditions it faces.

4.2 VRIO Analysis in Assessing Competitive Advantage

Understanding VRIO Analysis

VRIO analysis is a model used to evaluate a company's resources and capabilities to determine whether an organization has a sustainable competitive advantage. This model was developed by **Jay Barney (1991)** in **the Resource-Based View (RBV) theory** .

VRIO stands for four main dimensions:

1. **Value:** Does this resource provide value to the company?
2. **Rarity:** Is this resource rare or difficult for competitors to obtain?
3. **Imitability:** How difficult is this resource for competitors to copy?
4. **Organization:** Does the company have the systems and structures to utilize these resources effectively?

By using VRIO, companies can assess whether their assets and capabilities can provide a lasting competitive advantage.

VRIO Analysis Components

1. **Value (Value)**

- Resources must create value for the company by helping to increase efficiency or effectiveness.
- If a resource does not provide added value, then the company must consider alternative strategies.
- **Example:** Advanced technology in Amazon's supply chain improves shipping efficiency, providing a competitive advantage.

1. **Rarity**

- Rare resources provide a competitive advantage because they are not possessed by many competitors.
- If many companies have the same resources, then it becomes just a requirement to compete, not an advantage.
- **Example:** Apple's product design expertise is difficult for competitors to imitate, creating a unique appeal for consumers.

1. **Imitability (Can be imitated)**

- If a resource is easily imitated, competitors will quickly imitate it and eliminate the competitive advantage.

- Barriers to imitation can be high costs, complexity, or patents.
- **Example:** Coca-Cola's secret formula is a difficult-to-imitate resource that provides unique product differentiation.

1. **Organization (Organization)**

- Companies must have systems, culture and structures that support optimal utilization of resources.
- If a company does not have a good system, even if it has strong resources, competitive advantage will not be realized.
- **Example:** Toyota uses the **Lean Manufacturing production system** , which ensures optimal utilization of its technological and process advantages.

Competitive Advantage Evaluation Based on VRIO

- **If all four factors are met** , then the company has **a sustainable competitive advantage.**
- **If only some are fulfilled** , then the company only has **a temporary competitive advantage.**
- **If none of these are met** , the company does not have a competitive advantage and needs to innovate or restructure its strategy.

Application of VRIO Analysis in Business Strategy

1. **Identify Key Resources:** Companies need to identify assets or capabilities that can provide competitive advantage.
2. **Advantage Level Analysis:** Using VRIO to evaluate whether the resource is valuable, rare, difficult to imitate, and can be effectively utilized.
3. **Resource Management Strategy:** If a resource does not provide a competitive advantage, the company can:

- Increasing its value through innovation.

- Develop strategies to limit imitation by competitors.
- Improve the organizational structure to optimize its utilization.

Examples of VRIO Implementation in Companies in Indonesia

For example, **PT Gojek Indonesia** can be analyzed using the VRIO model:

- **Value:** Innovative application technology makes it easier for customers to get transportation services, digital payments, and food delivery.
- **Rarity:** Gojek has an integrated service ecosystem that not many competitors in the local market have.
- **Imitability:** Difficult to imitate due to extensive driver partner network, large investor support, and complex technological infrastructure.
- **Organization:** Gojek has a strong management system to develop and maintain its innovation and operations.

Because all four VRIO factors are met, Gojek has **a sustainable competitive advantage** that keeps it dominant in the digital services industry in Indonesia.

Conclusion

VRIO analysis is a very useful tool to assess whether a resource or capability can provide a sustainable competitive advantage for a company. By understanding and applying the VRIO model, companies can identify their strategic assets and develop more effective business strategies in the face of competition.

4.3 Value Chain Analysis

Understanding Value Chains

Value Chain Analysis was developed by **Michael Porter (1985)** as a tool to identify activities within an organization that can create added value and provide competitive advantage. The value chain describes how each business activity contributes to the company's strategic advantage.

According to Porter, the value chain consists of two main types of activities:

1. **Primary Activities:** Activities that are directly involved in creating a product or service and providing value to customers.
2. **Support Activities:** Activities that support the effectiveness and efficiency of primary activities.

By understanding how each activity creates value, companies can optimize their operations and increase competitive advantage.

Value Chain Components

1. Primary**Activities** Primary activities that are directly related to the production, distribution, and sale of products or services:

- **Inbound Logistics:** Management of raw materials and suppliers.
- **Operations:** The process of producing or providing services.
- **Outbound Logistics:** Distribution of products to customers.
- **Marketing & Sales:** Marketing and sales strategies.
- **Service:** After sales customer support.

1. **Support Activities** Activitiesthat support primary activities to make them more efficient:

- **Procurement:** Procurement of raw materials and equipment.
- **Technology Development:** Technological innovation and business pro-

cess improvement.

- **Human Resource Management:** Recruitment, training, and management of human resources.
- **Firm Infrastructure:** Corporate management, finance, and information systems.

If these activities are managed well, companies can improve their operational efficiency and competitive advantage.

Application of Value Chain Analysis in Business Strategy

1. **Increase Efficiency and Cost Reduction**

- Companies can identify inefficient processes and reduce production costs.
- Example: A manufacturing company implements **Lean Manufacturing** to increase productivity and reduce waste.

1. **Product and Service Differentiation**

- Leveraging value-added activities to improve the quality of products or services.
- Example: Apple uses premium design and technological innovation to differentiate its products from competitors.

1. **Optimizing the Use of Technology**

- Companies can improve value chain efficiency by adopting the latest technologies.
- Example: Amazon relies on AI-based logistics systems to optimize distribution of goods.

1. **Sustainable Competitive Advantage**

- Developing unique business processes that are difficult for competitors to imitate.
- Example: Toyota implements the **Toyota Production System (TPS)** to ensure high efficiency and the best product quality.

Examples of Value Chain Application in Companies in Indonesia

For example, **PT Indofood Sukses Makmur Tbk** can be analyzed using the value chain:

- **Inbound Logistics:** Indofood has an extensive and efficient raw material supply chain.
- **Operations:** Modern production plant with high production capacity.
- **Outbound Logistics:** A national distribution system that reaches all corners of Indonesia.
- **Marketing & Sales:** Aggressive marketing strategies and strong branding.
- **Service:** Good customer service and product innovation that suits market tastes.

By successfully optimizing every activity in its value chain, Indofood remains the market leader in the food industry in Indonesia.

Conclusion

Value Chain Analysis helps companies understand how each activity in their business creates added value. By implementing the right strategies, companies can increase efficiency, reduce costs, and strengthen their competitive advantage in the market.

4.4 Company Performance and Success Indicators

Understanding Company Performance

Company performance is a measure of an organization's success in achieving its strategic goals. Performance evaluation is conducted to assess the effectiveness of the strategies that have been implemented and to identify areas that need improvement.

According to Kaplan and Norton (1996), company performance can be measured through **the Balanced Scorecard (BSC)** which includes four main perspectives:

1. **Finance:** Measuring profitability, cost efficiency, and achievement of financial targets.
2. **Customers:** Assess customer satisfaction, loyalty, and market share.
3. **Internal Business Processes:** Analyze the company's operational efficiency, innovation, and productivity.
4. **Learning and Growth:** Evaluate HR capabilities, organizational culture, and the technology used.

Company Performance Success Indicators

To assess a company's long-term success, several key indicators are used, including:

1. **Financial Indicators**

- **Return on Investment (ROI):** Standard $\geq$ 15% for healthy companies, below 5% is considered less profitable.
- **Net Profit Margin:** Industry standards range from 10%–20% depending on the business sector.
- **Current Ratio:** A healthy ratio is usually above 1.5 to indicate sufficient liquidity.

1. **Customer Indicators**

- **Customer Satisfaction Index (CSI):** A customer satisfaction index above 80% is considered very good.
- **Customer Retention Rate:** Customer retention above 75% indicates high customer loyalty.
- **Brand Loyalty:** Market share of more than 50% in a target segment indicates brand dominance.

1. **Internal Business Process Indicators**

- **Cycle Time Reduction:** A reduction in production cycle time of $\geq$ 20% indicates increased efficiency.
- **Operational Efficiency:** Operational efficiency standards are targeted at above 85%.
- **Product Innovation Rate:** Companies that launch at least 3 innovative products per year demonstrate high competitiveness.

1. **Learning and Growth Indicators**

- **Employee Turnover Rate:** Turnover below 10% indicates good workforce stability.
- **Training Hours per Employee:** An average of over 40 hours of training per year indicates a good HR investment.
- **Technology Adoption Rate:** Companies with more than 70% of technology-based business processes demonstrate digitalization

readiness.

Implementation of Performance Evaluation in Business Strategy

1. **Identifying Critical Success Factors (CSFs):** The company must determine the key factors that contribute to achieving its business goals.
2. **Using a Comprehensive Measurement System:** A combination of financial and non-financial indicators is necessary for more accurate performance evaluation.
3. **Adjusting Strategy Based on Performance Evaluation:** If a strategy does not provide optimal results, the company needs to adjust or change its business strategy.
4. **Using Technology in Performance Monitoring:** ERP (Enterprise Resource Planning) systems and analytical dashboards can be used to automate performance measurement.

Examples of Implementation of Performance Evaluation in Indonesian Companies

For example, **PT Bank Rakyat Indonesia (BRI)** uses **the Balanced Scorecard (BSC) approach** to evaluate its performance:

- **Finance:** BRI targets net profit growth and operational cost efficiency.
- **Customers:** Improving customer satisfaction through digitalization of banking services.
- **Internal Business Process:** Accelerate the credit approval process for MSMEs to increase accessibility of financial services.
- **Learning and Growth:** Developing employee competencies through digital training programs and leadership development.

By using this indicator-based evaluation, BRI can improve operational efficiency, customer satisfaction, and its competitiveness in the banking industry.

Conclusion

Company performance evaluation is very important in ensuring that business strategies are running according to the goals set. By implementing **the Balanced Scorecard (BSC)** and other success indicators, companies can identify areas of improvement and optimize their competitive advantages.

Case Study: Competitive Advantage of Local Companies

Background

PT XYZ is a local electronics manufacturing company that has been operating for more than 20 years in Indonesia. Initially, the company focused on producing household appliances such as televisions and refrigerators. However, in recent years, PT XYZ has faced increasing competition from multinational companies such as Samsung and LG, which offer products with more advanced technology and competitive prices.

Although PT XYZ has a strong reputation in the domestic market, the company is starting to experience a decline in market share due to a lack of technological innovation and limited financial resources. Management realizes that the company needs to conduct an internal environmental analysis to identify competitive advantages that can be utilized to survive and grow.

Problems Faced

1. **Resources and Capabilities:**

- PT XYZ has an extensive distribution network in Indonesia, but still relies on imported raw materials.
- Limited funds for research and development (R&D) result in products that are less innovative.

1. **VRIO Analysis:**

- PT XYZ's brand is quite well-known in Indonesia (**Value**), but is still lacking in terms of technological innovation compared to global competitors.
- A wide distribution network is an advantage (**Rarity**), but is not yet supported by optimal digitalization.
- Manufacturing technology can still be imitated by competitors (**Imitability**), so companies need to look for other advantages that are difficult to imitate.
- The organization has a fairly strong management system (**Organization**), but still needs to improve operational efficiency.

1. **Value Chain:**

- **Inbound Logistics:** Dependence on imported raw materials results in high production costs.
- **Operations:** Production efficiency needs to be improved with more modern manufacturing technology.
- **Marketing & Sales:** Marketing strategies have not fully utilized e-commerce and digital marketing.
- **Service:** After-sales service still needs to be improved to be more competitive than global competitors.

1. **Company Performance and Success Indicators:**

- **Return on Investment (ROI)** is below the industry standard (8% compared to an average of 15%).
- **The Customer Satisfaction Index (CSI)** is at 75%, indicating that there is room for improvement in customer satisfaction.
- **Operational Efficiency** only reached 70%, while competing companies reached 85%.

Student Assignment

As a business strategy analyst, you are asked to help PT XYZ in developing a more effective strategy by answering the following questions:

1. **VRIO Analysis**

- Identify which resources or capabilities can be developed into sustainable competitive advantages for PT XYZ.
- What are your recommendations to improve the company's competitive position based on VRIO analysis?

1. **Value Chain**

- How can PT XYZ improve efficiency in its value chain to lower production costs and increase customer satisfaction?
- Recommend improvement strategies in each key activity in PT XYZ's value chain.

1. **Implementable Business Strategies**

- Recommend innovation and digitalization strategies that PT XYZ can implement to increase competitiveness.
- How can companies leverage e-commerce and digital marketing to expand their market share?

1. **Strategy Evaluation and Implementation**

- How does PT XYZ evaluate the effectiveness of the strategies implemented?
- What key success indicators should be used to assess the impact of the implemented strategy?

Expected Output:

- Strategy analysis report covering VRIO and Value Chain.
- Recommended business strategies that can be implemented by PT XYZ.
- A short presentation on solutions that can be implemented by PT XYZ.

CHAPTER 5: Strategy Formulation

5.1 Concept and Process of Strategy Formulation

Understanding Strategy Formulation

Strategy formulation is the process of developing strategic steps that will be used by a company to achieve competitive advantage. This process includes identifying organizational goals, analyzing the internal and external environment, and selecting the strategy that best suits the company's conditions.

According to David (2020), strategy formulation involves determining business direction, allocating resources, and making strategic decisions to create long-term value. Rivai & Prawironegoro (2019) added that strategy formulation must consider external factors (opportunities and threats) as well as internal factors (strengths and weaknesses) of the company.

Strategy Formulation Process

Strategy formulation consists of several main stages:

1. **Determining Vision, Mission, and Strategic Objectives**

- Determine the long-term direction of the company.
- Ensuring that the chosen strategy is in line with the organization's vision

and mission.

1. **External and Internal Environmental Analysis**

- **PESTEL** analysis and **Porter's Five Forces** to understand industry dynamics.
- **VRIO** and **Value Chain** analysis to assess internal strengths.

1. **Identify Alternative Strategies**

- Using **SWOT Analysis** to develop strategic options that can be taken.
- Leveraging **the TOWS Matrix** to align strategy with internal and external conditions.

1. **Choosing the Most Appropriate Strategy**

- Evaluate strategic alternatives using **Porter's Generic Strategy approach** (Differentiation, Low Cost, Focus).
- Choosing a strategy based on suitability with the company's resources and capabilities.

1. **Preparation of Strategy Implementation Plan**

- Design operational policies that support core strategies.
- Arrange optimal resource allocation to support implementation.

1. **Strategy Evaluation and Control**

- Using tools such as **the Balanced Scorecard** to monitor strategy effectiveness.
- Make strategy adjustments if necessary based on performance evaluation results.

The Importance of Strategy Formulation in Business Success

- **Enhancing Competitive Advantage:** The right strategy helps companies face competition and create value for customers.
- **Adapting to Environmental Changes:** Strategy formulation enables companies to adapt to industry dynamics and market trends.
- **Optimizing Resource Usage:** With a clear strategy, companies can allocate resources more efficiently.
- **Minimizing Business Risks:** A well-thought-out strategy formulation process helps reduce uncertainty and the risk of business failure.

Conclusion

Strategy formulation is a critical stage in strategic management that determines the direction and success of a company. By following a systematic and analysis-based process, organizations can develop effective and sustainable strategies to achieve their business goals.

5.2 SWOT Analysis as a Strategy Formulation Tool

Understanding SWOT Analysis

SWOT analysis is a method used in strategy formulation to evaluate **the Strengths, Weaknesses, Opportunities, and Threats** faced by an organization. This model helps companies understand their strategic position and develop effective strategies to increase competitive advantage.

According to David (2020), SWOT analysis provides a holistic view of internal and external factors that can affect company performance. Rivai & Prawironegoro (2019) added that a deep understanding of SWOT allows companies to adjust strategies to market conditions and available resources.

SWOT Analysis Components

1. **Strengths (Strengths)**

- Resources or capabilities that provide a company with a competitive advantage.
- Examples: Strong brand reputation, extensive distribution network, innovative technology.

1. **Weaknesses**

- Internal factors that inhibit company growth.
- Examples: Limited capital, outdated technology, dependence on a single supplier.

1. **Opportunities**

- External trends that can be leveraged for business growth.
- Examples: Changing customer preferences, development of new technologies, global market expansion.

1. **Threats (Threats)**

- External factors that can hinder a company's growth or profitability.
- Examples: Fierce competition, increasingly stringent regulations, changes in global economic conditions.

Steps to Using SWOT Analysis in Strategy Formulation

1. **Identifying Internal and External Factors**

- Using data from financial reports, customer surveys, and industry analysis.

1. **Analyzing and Mapping SWOT Factors**

- Compile a list of the company's strengths and weaknesses from an internal perspective.
- Determine opportunities and threats based on external factors.

1. **Developing Strategies Based on SWOT Findings**

- Developing **SO (Strength-Opportunity) strategies:** Utilizing strengths to take advantage of opportunities.
- Developing a **WO (Weakness-Opportunity) strategy:** Reducing weaknesses by taking advantage of opportunities.
- Developing **ST (Strength-Threat) strategy:** Using strengths to overcome threats.
- Develop a **WT (Weakness-Threat) strategy:** Minimize weaknesses to reduce the impact of threats.

Examples of Applying SWOT Analysis in Business

For example, here is a SWOT analysis for **PT Unilever Indonesia:**
From this analysis, PT Unilever Indonesia can implement **SO strategy** by increasing e-commerce penetration and introducing more environmentally friendly products. **WT strategy** can be operational cost efficiency to reduce the impact of exchange rate fluctuations.

Conclusion

SWOT analysis is a very useful tool in strategy formulation because it helps companies understand the strengths, weaknesses, opportunities, and threats they face. By using SWOT analysis effectively, companies can develop more adaptive and data-driven strategies to increase their competitiveness in the marketplace.

5.3 TOWS Matrix in Developing Strategy

Understanding the TOWS Matrix

TOWS matrix is a more systematic development of **SWOT analysis in formulating strategies. This concept was developed by Heinz Weihrich (1982)** to help organizations connect internal factors (**Strengths and Weaknesses**) with external factors (**Opportunities and Threats**) in a more effective strategy formulation process.

The TOWS matrix is used to:

- Identify strategies that can leverage **strengths** to capture **opportunities** .
- Adapting weaknesses to take advantage of available opportunities.
- Using existing strengths to confront external threats.
- Minimize weaknesses so as not to be affected by threats.

TOWS Matrix Structure

Steps for Preparing a TOWS Matrix

1. **Identify the company's SWOT factors.**

- Determine strengths (S), weaknesses (W), opportunities (O), and threats (T) based on internal and external data.

1. **Connect each SWOT factor in the TOWS matrix.**

- Create a combination of strategies that take advantage of the relationship between internal and external factors.

1. **Choose the strategy that best suits your company.**

- Prioritize strategies based on fit with resources and business conditions.

Examples of TOWS Matrix Implementation in Companies in Indonesia

For example, here is the application of the TOWS Matrix for **PT Unilever Indonesia:**

SWOT Factors of PT Unilever Indonesia:

- **Strengths (Strengths):**
- A strong and widely recognized brand.
- Extensive national distribution network.
- High product innovation capability.
- **Weaknesses:**
- Dependence on imported raw materials.
- High operating costs.
- Price competition with cheaper local products.
- **Opportunities:**
- The growing trend of eco-friendly products.
- Consumer lifestyle changes to healthy and natural products.
- Expansion of the e-commerce market in Indonesia.
- **Threats (Threats):**
- Competition with cheaper local brands.
- Regulatory uncertainty regarding imported raw materials.
- Rapid changes in market trends.

TOWS Strategy for PT Unilever Indonesia:

1. **SO (Strength-Opportunity) Strategy:**

- Leveraging brand power to develop an organic and eco-friendly product line.
- Using a wide distribution network to expand the market for sustainability-based products.
- Collaborate with e-commerce platforms to increase market penetration.

1. **ST (Strength-Threat) Strategy:**

- Increasing premium product innovation to maintain market share against local competitors.
- Ensuring regulatory compliance by building partnerships with local raw material suppliers.
- Implement a stronger branding strategy to face competition with local products.

1. **WO (Weakness-Opportunity) Strategy:**

- Reducing dependence on imported materials by seeking alternative local raw materials that are more competitive.
- Increase production efficiency to reduce operational costs while maintaining product quality.
- Taking advantage of the healthy product trend by developing products made from natural ingredients.

1. **WT (Weakness-Threat) Strategy:**

- Develop supply chain efficiency strategies to reduce costs and dependence on imported raw materials.
- Diversifying products to reduce risks in the event of changes in raw material regulations.
- Improving marketing effectiveness to maintain competitiveness in the domestic market.

Benefits of Using the TOWS Matrix

- **Facilitates the development of business strategies** with a more systematic approach.
- **Assists in decision making** by directly linking internal and external factors.
- **Increase company competitiveness** by developing strategies that are more adaptive to changes in the business environment.

Conclusion

The TOWS Matrix is a very effective strategy formulation tool in linking SWOT factors and creating a more targeted business strategy. By using this approach, companies can more easily adjust their strategies to the internal and external conditions they face.

5.4 Porter's Generic Strategy Model

Understanding Porter's Generic Strategy Model

Porter's Generic Strategy Model was introduced by **Michael Porter (1985)** as a framework to help companies build competitive advantage. This model suggests that companies can choose one of three main strategies to achieve a strong position in the market:

1. **Differentiation Strategy** – Focus on creating unique value in products or services.
2. **Low Cost Strategy (Cost Leadership Strategy)** – Offering products at lower prices than competitors.
3. **Focus Strategy** – Targeting a specific market segment with differentiation or low cost.

Porter's Types of Generic Strategies

1. **Differentiation Strategy**

- The company focuses on product innovation and high-quality services.
- Strong brands and customer experience are key strengths.
- Example: **Apple Inc.** which offers innovative designs and an exclusive product ecosystem.

1. **Low Cost Strategy**

- Companies reduce production costs to sell at lower prices than competitors.
- Operational efficiency and economies of scale are the keys to success.
- Example: **Indofood** produces instant noodles in large quantities at low cost.

1. **Focus Strategy**

- Companies target specific market segments, either through differentiation or low cost.
- These strategies can be divided into:
- **Focus Differentiation:** Unique products for niche markets (example: Tesla in the premium electric car segment).
- **Focus Cost Leadership:** Offering cheap products in certain segments (example: Alfamart in minimarket retail).

Application of Porter's Generic Strategy in Business

The following is an example of the application of Porter's generic strategy in **PT Gojek Indonesia:**

Advantages and Challenges of Each Strategy

Conclusion

Porter's Generic Strategy Model helps companies determine how to compete effectively in the market. By choosing a strategy that fits internal capabilities and market conditions, companies can create a sustainable competitive advantage.

Case Study: Strategy Formulation in a Start-Up Company

Background

PT TechStar is a start-up company engaged in financial technology (fintech). This company was founded with the aim of providing more efficient and secure digital payment solutions for the people of Indonesia. Currently, PT TechStar is facing challenges in developing its business amidst fierce competition with large fintech companies such as OVO, GoPay, and Dana.

Despite having innovative features in the form of blockchain technology to improve transaction security, PT TechStar is still struggling to gain significant market share. Limited marketing funds and low brand awareness are the main obstacles that must be overcome.

Problems Faced

1. **Competitive Advantage:** PT TechStar has blockchain technology that is more secure than its competitors, but it is not yet widely known by the public.
2. **Marketing Strategy:** Low brand awareness and limited marketing budget limit the growth of new users.
3. **Funding and Scalability:** The company is still dependent on early investors and needs to find a more sustainable funding strategy.

4. **Regulation:** Changes in government regulations regarding the fintech industry can impact business operations.

Student Assignment

As a business strategy analyst, you are asked to assist PT TechStart in developing a more effective strategy formulation by answering the following questions:

1. **SWOT Analysis and TOWS Matrix**

- Identify the strengths, weaknesses, opportunities and threats that PT TechStart has.
- Use **the TOWS Matrix** to develop strategies that can help your company address challenges and take advantage of opportunities.

1. **Application of Porter's Generic Strategy Model**

- Of Porter's three generic strategies (Differentiation, Low Cost, Focus), which strategy is most appropriate for PT TechStart? Explain your reasons.
- How can a company increase its competitive advantage with the chosen strategy?

1. **Digital Marketing Strategy and Market Expansion**

- How can PT TechStart increase brand awareness with a limited marketing budget?
- Recommend effective digital marketing strategies for PT TechStart.

1. **Strategy Evaluation and Implementation**

- What indicators of success can be used to evaluate the effectiveness of the strategies implemented?

- How does PT TechStart adjust its strategy if market conditions change?

Expected Output:

- Strategic analysis report that includes SWOT and TOWS.
- Recommended business strategies that can be implemented by PT Tech-Start.
- A short presentation on the solutions that can be implemented by PT TechStart.

CHAPTER 6: Business and Corporate Strategy

6.1 Differentiation and Low Cost Strategy

Understanding Differentiation Strategy and Low Cost

Business strategies can be categorized into two main approaches, namely **differentiation strategy** and **low-cost strategy** . Both of these strategies are ways for companies to build competitive advantage in the market.

1. **Differentiation Strategy**

- Companies try to create products or services that are unique and different from competitors.
- Differentiation can be achieved through technological innovation, superior quality, exclusive design, premium customer service, or a strong brand image.
- This strategy allows companies to set **premium prices** , because customers are willing to pay more for superior products.
- Example: **Apple** , which relies on proprietary designs and technological innovation to differentiate its products from competitors.

1. **Low Cost Strategy**

- Companies try to reduce production and operational costs in order to offer lower prices than competitors.
- This strategy focuses on production efficiency, supply chain optimization, and economies of scale.
- Companies that successfully implement a low-cost strategy can win price competition without sacrificing significant profit margins.
- Example: **Indofood** , which produces instant noodles in large quantities with efficient production costs.

Approaches in Differentiation Strategy

Differentiation strategy can be carried out through the following aspects:

1. **Product Differentiation:** Offering unique features or product advantages that competitors do not have.

- Example: Samsung with its foldable screen innovation on smartphones.

1. **Service Differentiation:** Providing the best customer service that increases consumer loyalty.

- Example: Amazon with fast shipping service and flexible return policy.

1. **Brand Differentiation:** Building an exclusive image that sticks in the minds of customers.

- Example: Rolex as a symbol of luxury in the watch industry.

Approaches in Low Cost Strategy

Low cost strategies can be achieved in several ways:

1. **Production Efficiency:** Using technology to increase productivity and reduce production waste.

- Example: Toyota with its **Lean Manufacturing production system** to reduce waste.

1. **Economies of Scale:** Producing in large quantities to lower costs per unit.

- Example: Walmart buys in bulk to keep prices down from suppliers.

1. **Supply Chain Optimization:** Reduce logistics costs with an efficient distribution system.

- Example: Amazon uses warehouse automation to speed up the shipping process.

Advantages and Challenges of Differentiation Strategy

Advantages and Challenges of Low Cost Strategy

Case Study: Differentiation Strategy and Low Cost in Indonesia

- **Differentiation Strategy: Garuda Indonesia** offers a premium flight experience with world-class service to differentiate itself from other airlines.
- **Low Cost Strategy: Lion Air** focuses on cost efficiency and offers lower ticket prices to reach a wider market segment.

Conclusion

Differentiation and low-cost strategies have their own advantages. Companies must choose the strategy that best suits their resources and target market. In some cases, companies can also combine both strategies to gain a stronger competitive advantage.

6.2 Integration and Diversification Strategy

Understanding Integration and Diversification Strategy

Integration and diversification strategies are two main approaches that companies use to expand their business, increase competitiveness, and reduce business risks.

1. **Integration Strategy**

- This strategy focuses on greater control over the supply or distribution chain to increase efficiency and competitiveness.
- This can be done through **Vertical Integration** (up or down the supply chain) and **Horizontal Integration** (acquiring competitors in the same industry).

1. **Diversification Strategy**

- Companies enter new markets or develop new products to reduce dependence on one line of business.
- Consists of **Related Diversification** (entering related industries) and **Unrelated Diversification** (entering different industries from the core

business).

Types of Integration Strategies

1. **Downstream Vertical Integration (Forward Integration)**

- The company takes over the distribution or sales of its own products.
- Example: Apple opened **Apple Store retail stores** to sell its products directly without intermediaries.

1. **Upstream Vertical Integration (Backward Integration)**

- The company acquires or controls suppliers of raw materials or components.
- Example: Tesla produces its own batteries for its electric vehicles to reduce dependence on suppliers.

1. **Horizontal Integration**

- Companies acquire or merge with competitors in the same industry to strengthen their market position.
- Example: Facebook's acquisition of Instagram to expand its dominance in social media.

Types of Diversification Strategies

1. **Related Diversification**

- The company enters into businesses that are still related to its core industry.
- Example: **Unilever** , which initially focused on food products, then entered

the personal care products business.

1. **Unrelated Diversification**

- Companies enter completely different industries to reduce market risk.
- Example: **Salim Group** which has businesses in the food, property and banking sectors.

Advantages and Challenges of Integration and Diversification Strategy

Case Study: Integration and Diversification Strategy in Indonesia

- **Vertical Integration: Astra International** has a vehicle production line, distribution, and after-sales service.
- **Related Diversification: Garuda Indonesia** which develops cargo and tourism service businesses.
- **Unrelated Diversification: Lippo Group** , which has businesses in the health, property and retail sectors.

Conclusion

Integration and diversification strategies allow companies to grow faster, reduce risk, and increase competitiveness. However, this strategy requires careful planning so as not to disrupt profitability and operational efficiency.

6.3 Strategic Alliances and Acquisitions

Understanding Strategic Alliances and Acquisitions

Strategic alliances and acquisitions are two major strategies that companies use to expand their business reach, increase competitiveness, and accelerate growth.

1. **Strategic Alliance**

- A form of cooperation between two or more companies to achieve common goals without carrying out a merger or acquisition.
- Strategic alliances can take the form of joint ventures, technology partnerships, or distribution collaborations.
- Example: **Gojek and Tokopedia** formed the GoTo Group to strengthen their digital ecosystem.

1. **Acquisition**

- The process by which one company buys most or all of the shares of another company to gain complete control.
- Acquisitions can be made to eliminate competitors, acquire new technology, or expand market share.
- Example: **Facebook acquired WhatsApp** to strengthen its dominance in the digital communications sector.

Types of Strategic Alliances

1. **Joint Venture**

- The new company was formed by two parent companies with joint ownership and responsibility.
- Example: **Sony Ericsson** , an alliance between Sony and Ericsson in the mobile phone industry.

1. **Non-Equity Alliance**

- Forms of cooperation without share ownership, such as distribution agreements or technology sharing.
- Example: **Starbucks partners with Nestlé** to distribute Starbucks coffee products in global supermarkets.

1. **Equity Alliance**

- One company owns shares in the partner company to strengthen long-term cooperation.
- Example: **Microsoft has a stake in OpenAI** to support the development of artificial intelligence technology.

Types of Acquisitions

1. **Horizontal Acquisition**

- Companies buy competitors in the same industry to increase market share.
- Example: **Facebook's acquisition of Instagram** to strengthen its social media dominance.

1. **Vertical Acquisition**

- Companies purchase suppliers or distributors to control the supply chain.
- Example: **Tesla acquired a battery supplier to ensure the availability of a key component for its electric vehicles.**

1. **Conglomerate Acquisition**

- Acquisition of companies in different industries for business diversification.
- Example: **Amazon acquired Whole Foods** to enter the food retail sector.

Advantages and Challenges of Strategic Alliances and Acquisitions

Case Study: Strategic Alliances and Acquisitions in Indonesia

- **Strategic Alliances: Gojek and Tokopedia** formed the GoTo Group to strengthen their competitiveness in the e-commerce and ride-hailing sectors.
- **Acquisition: Bank BCA acquires Bank Royal Indonesia** to expand digital banking services.

Conclusion

Strategic alliances and acquisitions are effective strategies for expanding a business and increasing a company's competitiveness. However, both strategies require careful planning and execution in order to provide maximum benefits to the companies involved.

6.4 Blue Ocean Strategy

Understanding Blue Ocean Strategy

Blue Ocean Strategy was introduced by **W. Chan Kim and Renée Mauborgne (2005)** in their book *Blue Ocean Strategy* . This concept emphasizes creating new, untapped markets (**Blue Ocean**) rather than competing in a market already full of intense competition (**Red Ocean**).

In a **Red Ocean strategy** , companies compete in existing markets, trying to outperform competitors by offering lower prices or better features. In contrast, in **a Blue Ocean** , companies create new demand by offering innovative value that has not existed before.

Blue Ocean Strategy Principles

1. **Creating New Market Space** – Focus on innovation and avoid direct competition.
2. **Increase Customer Value** – Provide a product or service with greater value than existing options.
3. **Reducing or Eliminating Unnecessary Factors** – Eliminating aspects that do not provide significant value to customers.
4. **Increasing Cost Efficiency** – The resulting innovation does not always require high costs, but rather resource optimization.

Blue Ocean Strategy Framework: Four Actions Framework

To create a Blue Ocean strategy, companies can use **the Four Actions Framework** , namely:

1. **Eliminate (Eliminate)** – Factors that are considered irrelevant or do not provide value to customers.
2. **Reduce (Reduce)** – Factors that are excessive compared to industry standards.
3. **Raise (Increase)** – Factors that need to be increased to create more value for customers.
4. **Create** – New elements that have never existed in the market.

Examples of Blue Ocean Strategy Implementation

Advantages and Challenges of Blue Ocean Strategy

Case Study: Implementation of Blue Ocean in Indonesia

- **Gojek** : Creating a new market by presenting an application-based online transportation service that previously did not exist in Indonesia.
- **Traveloka** : Makes it easier to book flight tickets and hotels with an online

system, eliminating dependence on conventional travel agents.

- **Tokopedia** : Connecting sellers and buyers without having to have a physical store, creating an e-commerce market that previously had not developed rapidly.

Conclusion

Blue Ocean strategy allows companies to create competitive advantage by avoiding direct competition. With the right innovation, companies can open new markets, increase customer value, and achieve higher profitability than conventional strategies.

Case Study: Multinational Company Diversification Strategy

Background

PT Global Corp is a multinational company engaged in various sectors, including food and beverage, electronics, and property. Initially, the company only focused on the food and beverage industry, but along with market developments and the need to expand its business reach, PT Global Corp began to diversify into other industries.

Diversification carried out by PT Global Corp includes expansion into the electronics industry by launching smart home appliance products. In addition, the company has also started investing in the property sector by building modern shopping centers and housing in various major cities in Indonesia and Southeast Asia.

Although this diversification strategy has brought significant growth, PT Global Corp faces several challenges, including difficulties in resource management, differences in regulations across sectors, and intense competition in the electronics and property industries.

Problems Faced

1. **Management Complexity:**

- Managing different business units requires a more complex management strategy.
- Coordination between business units is a major challenge in maintaining operational efficiency.

1. **Competition in New Industries:**

- In the electronics sector, PT Global Corp must compete with global brands such as Samsung and LG.
- In the property industry, companies face challenges from local developers who have more experience in the market.

1. **Regulation and Compliance:**

- Each industry has different regulations, which require compliance with certain standards.
- Adapting to changes in government policy is a major challenge in business expansion.

1. **Diversification Effectiveness:**

- Do the diversification steps taken really provide added value to the company?
- Are there any sectors that are more profitable to develop than the sectors currently being entered?

Student Assignment

As a business strategy analyst, you are asked to assist PT Global Corp in evaluating the diversification strategy that has been implemented and providing recommendations for future strategies by answering the following questions:

1. **Diversification Analysis**

- Based on the theory of diversification strategy, are the steps taken by PT Global Corp **related or unrelated diversification** ? Explain the reasons.
- What are the benefits and risks that companies face with this diversification model?

1. **Implementation of Integration Strategy**

- Should PT Global Corp implement **vertical or horizontal integration** in strengthening its diversification? Give reasons and examples of implementation.
- How can integration strategies improve a company's efficiency and competitiveness?

1. **Diversification Success Evaluation**

- How can PT GlobalCorp measure the success of its diversification strategy? State the key indicators that should be used.
- If you were the CEO of PT Global Corp, would you expand diversification into other industries or strengthen existing sectors? Explain the strategy you would take.

1. **Strategies for Facing Challenges**

- How can PT Global Corp overcome challenges in regulation and compliance across sectors?

- What strategies can companies implement to increase their competitiveness in the electronics and property industries?

Expected Output:

- PT Global Corp. diversification strategy analysis report
- Business strategy recommendations to improve company efficiency and competitiveness.
- A short presentation on strategic solutions for PT Global Corp.

CHAPTER 7: Strategy Implementation – Marketing Management

7.1 The Role of Marketing Strategy in Strategic Management

Understanding Marketing Strategy in Strategic Management

Marketing strategy is an integral part of strategic management that aims to create value for customers and ensure long-term business sustainability. Marketing strategy plays a role in connecting companies with the market through understanding customer needs, developing relevant products, and implementing effective marketing tactics.

According to Kotler & Keller (2020), marketing strategy is the process of designing and implementing marketing activities to achieve competitive advantage and business growth. This strategy must be aligned with the company's vision, mission, and strategic goals.

The Role of Marketing Strategy in Strategic Management

1. **Helping Companies in Differentiation**

- Marketing strategies allow companies to differentiate themselves from competitors through product innovation, customer service, and brand image.

- Example: Apple uses a differentiation strategy with premium product designs and an integrated service ecosystem.

1. **Targeting the Right Market**

- With proper market analysis, companies can determine the most potential customer segments.
- Example: Nike targets the athlete and sports enthusiast segment with high-quality products.

1. **Increase Brand Awareness**

- An effective marketing campaign helps companies increase brand visibility and appeal.
- Example: Coca-Cola with its global campaign that continues to strengthen its positive image in the eyes of consumers.

1. **Supporting Business Strategy Implementation**

- Marketing strategy is the main tool in implementing the formulated business strategy, be it differentiation, low cost, or focus strategy.
- Example: IKEA uses a marketing strategy that supports a low-cost business model with a unique shopping experience in its stores.

1. **Increase Customer Loyalty and Profitability**

- By understanding customer behavior and providing added value, companies can build long-term relationships with customers.
- Example: Starbucks has a loyalty program that encourages customers to keep coming back.

Key Components in Marketing Strategy

1. **Market Analysis:** Understanding industry trends, customer behavior, and competitor activities.
2. **Strategy Formulation:** Determining segmentation, targeting, and positioning (STP).
3. **Marketing Execution:** Using the appropriate marketing mix.
4. **Performance Evaluation:** Measure the effectiveness of marketing campaigns with KPI indicators such as marketing ROI and customer conversion rates.

Conclusion

Marketing strategy plays a central role in corporate strategy management as it helps in achieving competitive advantage, increasing brand awareness, and building customer loyalty. By implementing effective marketing strategies, companies can ensure sustainable growth and strong competitiveness in the industry.

Market Analysis in Marketing Strategy

Understanding Market Analysis

Market analysis is the process of collecting, evaluating, and interpreting information about the industry, customers, competitors, and external environmental factors that may affect a company's business strategy. By conducting market analysis, companies can understand industry trends, customer preferences, and opportunities and threats that may arise in the market.

Steps in Carrying Out Market Analysis

1. **Determining Market Analysis Objectives**

- Determine whether the analysis is being conducted for business expansion, new product launch, or competitive evaluation.
- Example: A company wants to know if there is a potential market for its innovative product.

1. **Identifying Target Market**

- Analyze who potential customers are based on their **demographics** , **geography** , **psychographics** , and **behavior** .
- Example: Premium beauty products target professional women aged 25–40 with high purchasing power.

1. **Analyzing Market Demand**

- Using data to understand market size, industry growth, and consumer behavior trends.
- Example: The increasing trend of healthy food consumption can be an opportunity for organic food businesses.

1. **Competitive Analysis**

- Using tools such as **Porter's Five Forces** to evaluate industry competitiveness.
- Examining competitors' competitive advantages and how their strategies can impact the business.
- Example: Analyze the e-commerce strategies used by major competitors in the fashion industry.

1. **Analyzing Trends and External Factors**

- Using **PESTEL Analysis** to understand the political, economic, social, technological, environmental and legal factors that affect the industry.
- Example: Changes in tax regulations for imported products can affect a company's pricing strategy.

1. **Determining Marketing Strategy Based on Analysis Results**

- Using the data obtained to design more effective marketing strategies.
- Example: If analysis shows that consumers are shopping more online, then the company needs to allocate a larger budget to digital marketing.

Tools Used in Market Analysis

1. **Customer Surveys and Interviews** – Collecting data directly from the target market.
2. **SWOT Analysis** – Identifying strengths, weaknesses, opportunities and threats in the market.
3. **Google Trends and Digital Analytics** – Understanding customer search patterns for a product.
4. **Secondary Data from Industry Reports** – Using market research reports to understand industry trends.

Conclusion

Market analysis is an essential element of marketing strategy that helps companies understand the dynamics of the industry, customers, and competitors. By conducting proper analysis, companies can develop more effective marketing strategies, increase competitiveness, and optimize opportunities in the market.

7.2 Segmentation, Targeting, and Positioning

Understanding Segmentation, Targeting, and Positioning (STP)

Segmentation, Targeting, and Positioning (**STP**) is an approach used by companies to determine the right customer segments, select the most profitable target market, and create the right brand position in the minds of consumers. The STP model helps companies develop more targeted and effective marketing strategies.

1. Market Segmentation

Market segmentation is the process of dividing a broad market into groups of customers with similar characteristics. Segmentation allows companies to understand customer needs and offer more appropriate products.

☑ **Types of Market Segmentation:**

1. **Demographic Segmentation:** Based on age, gender, income, education, occupation, etc.

- Example: Premium skincare products target women aged 25–40 years with high purchasing power.

1. **Geographic Segmentation:** Based on location such as city, state, or country.

- Example: Fast food companies offer different menus in each country to suit local tastes.

1. **Psychographic Segmentation:** Based on customer lifestyle, values, and personality.

- Example: A sportswear brand targets individuals who have an active and healthy lifestyle.

1. **Behavioral Segmentation:** Based on consumption patterns, loyalty, and purchase frequency.

- Example: A music streaming app targets customers based on music preferences and listening habits.

2. Targeting (Determining the Target Market)

After segmenting, the company needs to choose which segment is the most profitable to target as a market.
   ✔ **Targeting Strategy:**

1. **Mass Marketing:** Offering one product to the entire market without differentiation.

- Example: Basic necessities such as rice and salt.

1. **Segmented Marketing (Differentiated Marketing):** Offering different products to different segments.

- Example: An automotive company that provides cars for various economy classes.

1. **Niche Marketing (Focused Marketing):** Targeting a small segment with specific needs.

- Example: Luxury watches that only target executives.

1. **Micromarketing (Individual Marketing):** Tailoring products or services to specific individuals or communities.

- Example: Starbucks offers drink customization options according to customer preferences.

3. Positioning (Positioning the Brand in the Market)

Positioning is how a company builds a brand image in the minds of customers to differentiate itself from competitors.
   ✓ **Positioning Strategy:**

1. **Positioning Based on Price and Quality:**

- Example: Rolex is positioned as a premium watch with high quality.

1. **Positioning Based on Product Uniqueness:**

- Example: Tesla positions itself as an innovative and environmentally friendly electric car manufacturer.

1. **Positioning Based on Product Benefits:**

- Example: Sensodyne is positioned as a toothpaste specifically for sensitive teeth.

1. **Positioning Based on User or Lifestyle:**

- Example: Nike positions itself as a brand for athletes and physically active individuals.

Steps in Determining STP

1. **Market Analysis** – Using market research to understand customer needs.
2. **Market Segment Identification** – Dividing the market into customer groups based on certain characteristics.
3. **Market Potential Evaluation** – Determining which segments have the highest growth and profit potential.
4. **Selecting a Target Market** – Selecting the most profitable segment for the company.
5. **Determining Positioning Strategy** – Building a strong brand image in line with product values and advantages.
6. **Developing Marketing Strategy** – Developing marketing messages and campaigns that are relevant to the target market.

Conclusion

The Segmentation, Targeting, and Positioning (STP) model is an important strategy in marketing that allows companies to understand customers, select the most potential segments, and build a strong brand position. By implementing the right STP, companies can increase the effectiveness of their marketing strategies and win the competition in the market.

7.3 Marketing Mix Strategy

Understanding Marketing Mix

Marketing Mix or **marketing mix** is a combination of various marketing elements used by companies to achieve business goals and meet customer needs. This concept was first introduced by **E. Jerome McCarthy** in 1960 with the **4P model** , namely **Product, Price, Place, and Promotion** . Over time, this model has developed into **7P** with the addition **of People, Process, and Physical Evidence** for the service industry.

Elements in Marketing Mix

✓ 1. Product

- Products or services offered to customers must have added value and be able to meet market needs.
- Example: Apple designed the iPhone with innovative features to differentiate itself from competitors.

✓ 2. Price (Price)

- Pricing strategies must be in line with the value provided to customers and take into account market purchasing power.
- Example: Netflix uses a subscription pricing model with different tiers of service.

✓ 3. Place (Distribution)

- How products or services are delivered to customers, whether through physical stores, e-commerce, or other distribution networks.
- Example: Amazon uses an efficient distribution system with an extensive logistics network.

✓ 4. Promotion

- Communication strategies used to attract customers' attention, such as advertising, social media, and marketing campaigns.
- Example: Coca-Cola ran a global campaign with emotional and engaging advertising.

✓ 5. People

- Employees and salespeople who interact with customers and influence their experience with the brand.

- Example: Friendly customer service in luxury hotels increases guest loyalty.

✔ 6. Process (Process)

- Business processes that ensure customers have a good experience from purchase to after-sales service.
- Example: McDonald's has standard operational processes to ensure consistent food quality worldwide.

✔ 7. Physical Evidence

- Real evidence that can increase customer trust in a product or service, such as store design, product packaging, or customer testimonials.
- Example: Starbucks creates a comfortable cafe atmosphere to enhance customer experience.

The Importance of Marketing Mix in Marketing Strategy

1. **Adapting products to customer needs** – Optimizing products and services to suit market preferences.
2. **Optimizing pricing strategy** – Ensuring competitive prices while still providing benefits to the company.
3. **Improving distribution efficiency** – Ensuring products are easily accessible to targeted customers.
4. **Strengthening promotional strategies** – Using the right media to reach the appropriate target market.
5. **Improving customer satisfaction** – Ensuring services, processes and interactions with customers provide a positive experience.

Conclusion

Marketing Mix is an important element in marketing strategy that allows companies to achieve competitive advantage and attract customers. By optimizing the combination of **7Ps** , companies can create more value for customers and increase competitiveness in the market.

7.4 Implementation of Digital Marketing in Corporate Strategy

Understanding Digital Marketing

Digital marketing is a marketing strategy that utilizes digital technology and online platforms to reach customers more effectively. With the increasing use of the internet and mobile devices, digital marketing has become an essential part of modern marketing strategies.

According to Kotler & Keller (2020), digital marketing allows companies to interact directly with customers, increase engagement, and measure campaign effectiveness in real-time.

Key Components of Digital Marketing

☑ **1. Search Engine Optimization (SEO)**

- Optimize your website to appear on the first page of Google search results and other search engines.
- Example: Business blogs that implement SEO can increase organic traffic to their sites.

☑ **2. Content Marketing**

- Creation and distribution of quality content to attract and retain cus-

tomers.
- Example: An educational video on YouTube about the benefits of a product to increase brand awareness.

✅ 3. Social Media Marketing

- Leverage social media platforms like Instagram, Facebook, LinkedIn, and Twitter to engage with customers.
- Example: Starbucks uses Instagram for an engaging and interactive visual campaign.

✅ 4. Email Marketing

- Use of email to send promotions, newsletters, or direct communications to customers.
- Example: E-commerce sends emails with special discounts to customers who haven't shopped in a while.

✅ 5. Pay-Per-Click (PPC) Advertising

- Paid advertising on digital platforms such as Google Ads and Facebook Ads that are charged per click.
- Example: Shopee uses Google Ads to target customers searching for specific products online.

✅ 6. Affiliate Marketing & Influencer Marketing

- Work with affiliates or influencers to promote products.
- Example: Fashion brands collaborate with influencers to review products on their social media.

✅ 7. Marketing Automation

- The use of technology to automate marketing processes such as automated emails and chatbots.
- Example: A travel company uses chatbots to answer customer questions in real-time.

The Advantages of Digital Marketing in Corporate Strategy

1. **Wider Reach** – Able to reach customers in various locations without geographical limitations.
2. **Cost Efficiency** – More economical than traditional marketing such as television or print advertising.
3. **Real-Time Measurement** – Campaigns can be monitored and adjusted directly with analytics data.
4. **Direct Interaction with Consumers** – Enables more personal two-way communication.
5. **Increased Conversions** – The right strategy can increase customer conversion rates higher.

Challenges in Implementing Digital Marketing

1. **Fierce Competition** – Many businesses compete for customer attention in the digital world.
2. **Algorithm Changes** – Platforms like Google and social media frequently change algorithms that affect content visibility.
3. **Data Security and Privacy** – Companies must comply with regulations regarding customer data protection.
4. **Skills and Resources** – Digital marketing requires technical expertise and ever-evolving strategies.

Success Strategy in Digital Marketing

1. **Creating Valuable Content** – Interesting and useful content will more easily attract customers' attention.
2. **Using Data Analytics** – Optimize campaigns based on customer data analysis results.
3. **Optimizing Mobile Marketing** – Considering that the majority of internet users access information via mobile devices.
4. **Building an Online Community** – Using social media to build a loyal customer community.

Conclusion

Digital marketing is an important strategy in modern marketing that allows companies to reach a wider market at a more efficient cost. By utilizing the right technology, companies can increase customer engagement, build brand awareness, and optimize business results.

Case Study: Implementation of Digital Marketing Strategy in Indonesian Company

Background

PT E-Commerce Nusantara is one of the largest online retail companies in Indonesia that provides various products ranging from household needs to electronics. Along with the increasing competition in the e-commerce industry, PT E-Commerce Nusantara faces challenges in maintaining market share and increasing customer loyalty.

With the increasing number of e-commerce players in Indonesia, PT E-Commerce Nusantara needs to adopt innovative digital marketing strategies to increase market reach, strengthen brand image, and increase sales conversions.

Challenges Faced

1. **Fierce Competition in the Industry**

- Many e-commerce platforms offer similar services with massive promotions.
- The dominance of big brands such as Tokopedia, Shopee, and Lazada which have bigger marketing budgets.

1. **Changes in Consumer Behavior**

- Consumers are increasingly selective in choosing online shopping platforms.
- Increasing preference for more personal and interactive shopping experiences.

1. **Effectiveness of Digital Marketing Strategy**

- The challenge in optimizing digital advertising to be more efficient and not just rely on discount promotions.
- Ensuring that digital marketing strategies can deliver better conversion rates.

Implemented Digital Marketing Strategies

1. **Utilizing Big Data and AI in Marketing**

- Using **Artificial Intelligence (AI)** to analyze customer behavior and provide more personalized product recommendations.
- Example: AI-based product recommendation system displayed on the customer's homepage.

1. **SEO and SEM optimization**

- Increase visibility in search engines with SEO optimization on product descriptions and educational blogs.
- Using **Search Engine Marketing (SEM)** such as Google Ads to increase traffic to a website.

1. **Social Media Marketing Strategy**

- Using platforms like Instagram, TikTok, and Facebook to engage with customers.
- Influencer-based marketing campaigns to increase engagement and brand awareness.

1. **Email Marketing and Automation**

- Send personalized emails with special promotions to customers based on their shopping history.
- Using chatbots and marketing automation to increase customer engagement.

1. **Customer Loyalty and Retention Program**

- Providing rewards and cashback for customers who shop frequently.
- Using **gamification strategies** such as points programs to increase customer engagement.

Student Assignment

As a digital marketing strategy analyst, you are asked to evaluate the success of PT E-Commerce Nusantara's digital marketing strategy implementation and provide recommendations to improve its effectiveness. Answer the following questions:

1. **Strengths and Weaknesses Analysis**

- What are the advantages of the digital marketing strategy that has been implemented by PT E-Commerce Nusantara?
- What are the main weaknesses that still need to be fixed?

1. **Optimizing Digital Marketing Strategy**

- Which strategy do you think is most effective in increasing customer engagement?
- How can PT E-Commerce Nusantara optimize the use of AI and customer data to improve the online shopping experience?

1. **Evaluation of Digital Marketing Effectiveness**

- What indicators can be used to measure the success of a digital marketing strategy?
- How to increase **Return on Investment (ROI)** in digital marketing campaigns?

1. **Future Strategy Recommendations**

- How can PT E-Commerce Nusantara compete better with other large e-commerce companies?
- What digital marketing innovations can be implemented to increase customer loyalty in the long term?

Expected Output:

- Digital marketing strategy analysis report of PT E-Commerce Nusantara.
- More effective digital marketing strategy recommendations.
- A short presentation on strategic solutions for PT E-Commerce Nusantara.

CHAPTER 8: Strategy Implementation – Human Resource Management

8.1 The Role of HR in Strategy Implementation

Understanding Human Resource Management in Business Strategy

Human Resource Management (HR) has a key role in implementing a company's business strategy. Competent and skilled HR will ensure that the strategies that have been designed can be implemented effectively and achieve organizational goals.

According to **Dessler (2021)** , HR management involves the process of planning, recruiting, developing, and maintaining a workforce that is in accordance with the needs of the organization. Thus, HR not only plays a role in daily operations but also in creating long-term value for the company.

The Role of HR in Strategy Implementation

1. **Aligning Employee Competencies with Company Strategy**

- HR is responsible for ensuring that employees have the skills that match business needs.
- Example: Technology companies like Google provide artificial intelligence training to their employees to support product innovation.

1. **Increase Productivity and Efficiency**

- Human resource management develops more efficient work systems to increase productivity.
- Example: Implementation of a hybrid work system in a multinational company to increase work flexibility and work–life balance.

1. **Building a Strong Organizational Culture**

- A good organizational culture encourages employee engagement and commitment to the company's vision.
- Example: Netflix implements a work culture based on transparency and freedom in decision-making.

1. **Supporting Change and Innovation**

- HR plays a role in managing change, including the implementation of new technologies and business expansion strategies.
- Example: Amazon continues to drive innovation by training employees in automation and artificial intelligence.

1. **Ensuring Compliance with HR Regulations and Policies**

- Human Resource Management is responsible for ensuring compliance with employment regulations and business ethics.
- Example: Manufacturing companies must comply with occupational safety standards to protect employees.

HR Strategy in Strategic Management Implementation

To support the implementation of business strategies, companies can implement HR strategies as follows:

- **Recruitment and Selection Strategy:** Selecting talent that fits the company's needs.
- **Employee Development Strategy:** Providing training and career development.
- **Employee Retention Strategy:** Maintaining employee satisfaction and well-being to keep them productive.
- **Performance Management Strategy:** Measuring and evaluating employee achievement against company goals.

Conclusion

The role of HR in strategy implementation is very important to ensure alignment between business goals and workforce capabilities. With effective HR management, companies can achieve competitive advantage and ensure business sustainability amidst fierce competition.

8.2 Effective HR Management Strategies

Understanding Human Resource Management Strategy

An effective Human Resources (HR) management strategy aims to ensure that an organization's workforce has the skills, motivation, and capabilities needed to support the implementation of business strategies. Good HR management focuses not only on recruitment and selection, but also on employee development, retention, and performance improvement.

According to **Armstrong (2020)** , HR management strategies must be aligned with organizational goals and create competitive advantages through optimization of human resources.

Components of an Effective Human Resource Management Strategy

✓ 1. Strategy-Oriented Recruitment and Selection

- Ensuring the company recruits individuals who have skills and values that align with the organization's vision.
- Example: Technology companies like Google use competency and innovation-based selection processes to attract the best talent.

✓ 2. Continuous Employee Development

- Providing training and education to improve employee competency.
- Example: Amazon provides internal training programs to improve employees' digital and leadership skills.

✓ 3. KPI (Key Performance Indicators) Based Performance Management

- Develop an evaluation system based on achieving clear and measurable targets.
- Example: A company uses a **Balanced Scorecard- based assessment system** to measure employee productivity and effectiveness.

✓ 4. Employee Retention and Well-being

- Providing incentives, work-life balance, and a conducive work environment.
- Example: Companies like Netflix implemented **a work from anywhere policy** to increase employee flexibility.

✓ 5. Adaptive Organizational Culture Management

- Creating an innovative and inclusive organizational culture for employees to thrive.
- Example: Facebook encourages collaboration with an open and transparency-based work environment.

Human Resource Management Strategy in Supporting Business Implementation

1. **Workforce Planning:** Aligning the number and skills of the workforce with business needs.
2. **Leadership Development:** Developing future leaders through leadership programs.
3. **Employer Branding:** Increasing the attractiveness of a company as a desirable workplace.
4. **Digital HR Transformation:** Using technology in HR management for operational efficiency.

Challenges in Human Resource Management

- **Rapid Technological Change** → HR must always be up-to-date with technological developments.
- **Global Talent Competition** → Companies must be able to attract and retain the best talent.
- **Effective Performance Management** → Requires a data-based evaluation system and accurate metrics.

Conclusion

An effective HR management strategy is essential in implementing business strategies. By focusing on recruitment, development, performance management, and employee retention, companies can create a competitive and productive workforce. Good HR management will increase the competitiveness of the organization and drive long-term business sustainability.

8.3 Talent Management and Leadership Development

Understanding Talent Management and Leadership Development

Talent Management is a strategic approach to managing, developing, and retaining individuals with high potential to support business sustainability. Meanwhile, **Leadership Development** focuses on developing leadership skills so that employees can lead teams and organizations effectively.

According to **Berger & Berger (2020)** , talent management and leadership development are key factors in building a competitive and innovative organization.

Talent Management Components

✔ **1. Competency Based Recruitment and Selection**

- Ensuring the company gets individuals who have skills and values that match the organization's culture.
- Example: Tesla is recruiting engineers with high expertise in electric car technology to strengthen innovation.

✔ **2. Employee Development (Career Development)**

- Provide training and mentoring programs to improve employee competency.

- Example: Google has a "Grow with Google" program that focuses on improving employee skills.

✓ 3. Potential Based Performance Management

- Using an evaluation system to identify employees who have the potential to become future leaders.
- Example: General Electric (GE) implemented the **Nine-Box Grid model** to group employees based on their performance and potential.

✓ 4. Employee Retention and Well-being

- Offering competitive benefits and a work environment that supports employee well-being.
- Example: Netflix has a flexible leave policy to improve employee work-life balance.

Leadership Development Strategy

✓ 1. Leadership Training

- A training program designed to hone leadership, communication and decision-making skills.
- Example: IBM has a "Leadership Academy" to train future leaders.

✓ 2. Coaching and Mentorship

- Senior leaders mentor potential employees in developing managerial skills.

- Example: Microsoft implemented a **Reverse Mentoring program** , where younger generations mentor senior executives on new technology trends.

✅ 3. Job Rotation and Diverse Work Experience

- Provides experience across departments to broaden leadership perspectives.
- Example: Unilever implements a **Management Trainee program** , where participants gain work experience in various business units.

Challenges in Talent Management and Leadership Development

- **Limited Quality Talent** → Increasing competition to get the best talent.
- **Need for Continuous Development** → Companies must continuously adapt development strategies to industry trends.
- **High Talent Retention** → Avoid losing high performing employees due to lack of recognition and development opportunities.

Conclusion

Talent Management and Leadership Development are key elements in building an innovative and competitive organization. With the right strategy, companies can attract, develop, and retain talented individuals to ensure sustainable business growth.

8.4 Organizational Culture and Performance

Understanding Organizational Culture and Performance

Organizational culture is a set of values, beliefs, and norms that shape the way a company works and interacts. It plays a significant role in influencing employee behavior and the effectiveness of business strategies implemented.

According to **Schein (2017)** , organizational culture reflects the company's identity and has a major impact on motivation, productivity, and the success of implementing business strategies. Meanwhile, organizational performance refers to the achievement of business goals based on established indicators, such as revenue growth, operational efficiency, and customer satisfaction.

The Role of Organizational Culture in Improving Performance

✓ 1. Encourage Innovation and Creativity

- A culture that supports innovation helps companies create new solutions and increase competitiveness.
- Example: Google has an innovation-based work culture, where employees are given the freedom to develop creative projects.

✓ 2. Increase Employee Loyalty and Engagement

- A positive work environment increases employee engagement with the company and reduces turnover rates.
- Example: Zappos implemented a company culture based on employee satisfaction to increase loyalty.

✓ 3. Aligning Individual Goals with Corporate Strategy

- A strong organizational culture ensures that every employee works in accordance with the company's vision and mission.
- Example: Amazon implements a work culture based on speed and efficiency to increase customer satisfaction.

✓ 4. Increase Efficiency and Productivity

- A clear work system and strong company values help employees work more effectively.
- Example: Toyota uses a **Kaizen culture** that focuses on continuous improvement in company operations.

Key Elements in Organizational Culture

1. **Core Values:** The main principles that guide decision making.
2. **Norms and Behaviors:** Habits that are internalized by employees at work.
3. **Symbols and Rituals:** Company practices that reflect the organization's culture, such as employee awards and company events.
4. **Leadership Style:** The way management shapes and directs organizational culture.

Strategies for Building a Strong Organizational Culture

1. **Defining and Communicating Company Values** – Ensuring all employees understand and implement the organizational culture.
2. **Implementing Leadership that Promotes a Positive Culture** – Leaders must be role models in reflecting the desired work culture.
3. **Building a Reward and Recognition System** – Providing incentives for employees who contribute to achieving organizational goals.
4. **Conduct Periodic Evaluation and Adaptation** – Measure the effectiveness of organizational culture on company performance and make changes if necessary.

Challenges in Building a Strong Organizational Culture

- **Resistance to Change** → Employees who are used to the old culture may find it difficult to adapt.
- **Difficulty in Aligning Culture with New Strategy** → A culture that is not aligned with business strategy can hinder growth.
- **Cultural Differences in Global Organizations** → Multinational companies must be able to balance global and local cultures.

Conclusion

A strong organizational culture plays a vital role in determining the success of business strategy implementation and the achievement of company performance. By building a culture that is in line with the company's vision, organizations can increase productivity, employee loyalty, and competitiveness in the global market.

Case Study: HR Strategy in a Technology Company

Background

PT Tech Advance is a technology company engaged in the development of artificial intelligence (AI)-based software. In recent years, the company has experienced rapid growth due to the increasing demand for AI-based solutions. However, with rapid growth, PT Tech Advance faces challenges in managing human resources (HR) to ensure that business strategies can run effectively. Some of the major challenges faced by PT Tech Advance include:

- **Tech talent shortage** – The high demand for workers in the AI and data science fields has led to fierce competition in recruiting quality talent.
- **Low employee retention rates** – Talented employees often move to other

companies that offer higher salaries or better career opportunities.

- **Less adaptive work culture** – Companies still face resistance to change in adopting new technologies and agile work methods.
- **Lack of strong leadership** – The lack of leadership development programs makes it difficult for companies to develop future leaders.

HR Strategies Implemented

To overcome these challenges, PT Tech Advance implements several HR management strategies:

✓ **1. Competency Based Recruitment and Employer Branding**

- PT Tech Advance builds the company's image as an innovative workplace with an attractive environment for technology talents.
- Using competency-based recruitment methods and data analysis to find the best candidates.
- Example: Holding hackathons and scholarship programs to attract top graduates from top universities.

✓ **2. Employee Retention and Development Program**

- Provides additional benefits such as stock options, work flexibility, and modern work facilities.
- Implement employee development programs that focus on improving technical and leadership skills.
- Example: Offering a free AI certification program to upskill employees.

✓ **3. Strengthening Work Culture and Agile Adaptation**

- **agile** working methods to increase efficiency and flexibility in product development.

- Strengthening communication and transparency within the organization to build a collaborative work culture.
- Example: Hold a monthly "Innovation Friday" session to encourage employee creativity.

✓ 4. Leadership Development Program

- Identify and develop potential employees to become future leaders.
- Implementing mentoring and coaching for employees with high leadership potential.
- Example: Implementing **a Rotational Leadership Program** , where high potential employees are placed in various divisions for 6 months to broaden their horizons.

Student Assignment

As an HR strategy analyst, you are asked to evaluate the success of HR strategy implementation at PT Tech Advance and provide recommendations to improve the effectiveness of the strategy. Answer the following questions:

1. **Evaluation of Strengths and Challenges**

- What are the advantages of the HR strategy that PT Tech Advance has implemented?
- What are the main challenges that still need to be overcome in this company's HR management?

1. **Optimizing HR Strategy**

- Which strategies do you think are most effective in increasing employee retention and productivity?
- How can PT Tech Advance strengthen employer branding to attract more tech talents?

1. **Leadership Development and Organizational Culture**

- How can PT Tech Advance build an organizational culture that is more adaptive to change?
- What steps can be taken to accelerate leadership development in a company?

1. **Future Recommendations**

- If you were the Chief Human Resource Officer (CHRO) at PT Tech Advance, what strategies would you implement to improve the company's HR competitiveness?
- How can companies ensure that the HR strategies they implement remain relevant to future technological developments?

Expected Output:

- HR strategy analysis report of PT Tech Advance.
- Recommendations for HR management strategies to improve business effectiveness.
- A short presentation on strategic solutions for PT Tech Advance.

CHAPTER 9: Strategy Implementation – Operations & Production Management

9.1 Operations and Production Strategy in Competitive Advantage

Understanding Operations and Production Strategy

Operations and production strategy is an approach used by companies to manage production processes efficiently to create competitive advantage. This strategy includes resource management, quality improvement, and efficiency in the supply chain.

According to **Chase & Jacobs (2021)**, an effective operations strategy can increase productivity, reduce production costs, and ensure that the products or services produced meet customer expectations.

The Role of Operations Strategy in Competitive Advantage

✅ **1. Production Cost Efficiency**

- Optimizing operational costs through more efficient processes and proper use of resources.
- Example: Toyota implemented a **Just-In-Time (JIT) system** to reduce raw material waste and storage costs.

✓ 2. Improve Product Quality

- Focus on quality control to ensure that the products produced meet customer standards.
- Example: Samsung implements a **Total Quality Management (TQM) system** to ensure that each product meets high standards.

✓ 3. Production Speed and Flexibility

- Ensuring production processes can adapt quickly to changes in market demand.
- Example: Zara uses a **fast fashion production strategy** , where clothing collections can be produced and distributed in a short time.

✓ 4. Effective Supply Chain Management

- Managing relationships with suppliers and distributors to improve efficiency in the supply chain.
- Example: Amazon optimizes its supply chain with data-driven distribution systems and artificial intelligence.

✓ 5. Innovation in Production Process

- Adopting new technologies to increase productivity and reduce production costs.
- Example: Tesla uses **robotics and artificial intelligence** in its electric car manufacturing process.

Operational Strategies That Can Be Applied

1. **Make-to-Stock (MTS) Strategy:** Production in large quantities based on forecasted demand.
2. **Make-to-Order (MTO) Strategy:** Production is only carried out after receiving orders from customers.
3. **Mass Customization Strategy:** Combining mass production with customization based on customer demand.

Challenges in Implementing Operations Strategy

- **Market Demand Volatility** → Changes in market trends can affect production efficiency.
- **Dependence on Suppliers** → Delays in raw materials can hamper the production process.
- **Implementation of New Technologies** → Initial investment in technology often requires large costs.

Conclusion

Operations and production strategies play a vital role in creating competitive advantage through efficiency, quality, and innovation. Companies that are able to manage their operations well will have higher competitiveness and be able to face industry challenges better.

9.2 Lean Manufacturing and Six Sigma

Understanding Lean Manufacturing and Six Sigma

Lean Manufacturing and Six Sigma are two approaches used in operations management to improve production efficiency and reduce waste. Both methods focus on improving quality, efficiency, and productivity in the manufacturing process.

According to **Womack & Jones (2003)**, **Lean Manufacturing** is a systematic approach to eliminating waste in production without sacrificing quality. Meanwhile, **Six Sigma** is a data-driven method developed by **Motorola** and aims to improve quality by reducing variability in the production process.

Lean Manufacturing Concept

✔ 1. Eliminate Waste (Waste Reduction)

- Identify and eliminate activities that do not add value.
- Example: Toyota implemented **Just-In-Time (JIT)** to reduce excess inventory.

✔ 2. Increased Efficiency through Standardization

- Develop more effective work procedures to increase productivity.
- Example: McDonald's uses a standardized production system to ensure consistency across its stores.

✔ 3. Kaizen (Continuous Improvement)

- Prioritize continuous improvement in every aspect of production.
- Example: Electronics companies like Sony apply **Kaizen** in their product innovation.

✔ 4. Employee Empowerment

- Provide training and freedom for employees to contribute to improving work processes.
- Example: Manufacturing companies like Boeing involve production operators in improving work processes.

Six Sigma Concept

✓ 1. Focus on Reducing Variation

- Using statistical analysis to identify and reduce defects in production.
- Example: General Electric (GE) uses Six Sigma to improve operational efficiency.

✓ 2. DMAIC method (Define, Measure, Analyze, Improve, Control)

- **Define:** Identify the problem and objectives of the project.
- **Measure (Mengukur):** Collect data and measure process performance.
- **Analyze (Menganalyze):** Analyze data to find the root cause of the problem.
- **Improve:** Develop and implement improvement solutions.
- **Control (Control):** Ensuring that implemented improvements remain sustainable.

✓ 3. Reduction of Production Defects

- Improve product quality by reducing defect rates to **3.4 defects per million opportunities** .
- Example: A pharmaceutical company implements Six Sigma to ensure each production batch meets regulatory standards.

Differences between Lean Manufacturing and Six Sigma

The Benefits of Lean Manufacturing and Six Sigma in Operations

1. **Reducing Waste and Production Costs** – Ensuring operational efficiency.
2. **Improve Product Quality** – Reduce production defects and increase customer satisfaction.
3. **Improve Response to Market Demand** – Enables more flexible production.
4. **Increase Employee Engagement** – Encourage employees to participate in innovation and improvement.

Challenges in Lean and Six Sigma Implementation

- **Resistance to change** – Employees may have difficulty adapting to new processes.
- **Large initial investment** – Requires resources for training and equipment.
- **Complex performance measurement** – Requires accurate data for Six Sigma analysis.

Conclusion

Lean Manufacturing and Six Sigma are two key strategies in operations management that can improve production efficiency and product quality. With the right combination of these two approaches, companies can achieve a competitive advantage in an increasingly competitive market.

9.3 Supply Chain Management in Strategy Implementation

Understanding Supply Chain Management (SCM)

Supply Chain Management (SCM) is the process of planning, managing, and controlling the flow of goods, information, and resources from suppliers to end customers. Effective SCM enables companies to improve operational efficiency, reduce costs, and increase customer satisfaction.

According to **Christopher (2016)**, SCM is a strategic approach to coordinating various elements in the supply chain to create added value and increase the company's competitiveness.

Key Components in Supply Chain Management

✓ **1. Demand Management**

- Understand customer needs and plan production according to market demand.
- Example: Amazon uses AI technology to predict customer purchasing patterns and optimize inventory.

✓ **2. Inventory Management**

- Manage stock to avoid excess or shortage of goods.
- Example: Toyota implemented a **Just-In-Time (JIT) system** to avoid excessive inventory buildup.

✓ **3. Logistics and Distribution Management**

- Optimize the product delivery process from the warehouse to customers efficiently.
- Example: FedEx uses a real-time tracking system to ensure timely delivery.

✓ **4. Supplier Relationship Management**

- Building strategic partnerships with suppliers to ensure the availability of quality raw materials.
- Example: Apple works with key suppliers like TSMC to source high-quality components.

✅ 5. Technology in Supply Chain

- Utilizing ERP (Enterprise Resource Planning) systems and AI to automate supply chain management.
- Example: Walmart uses blockchain technology to increase transparency in its supply chain.

Supply Chain Management Strategy in Business Strategy Implementation

1. **Lean Supply Chain:** Eliminating waste and increasing efficiency in the supply chain.
2. **Agile Supply Chain:** Adapting a flexible supply chain to respond quickly to market changes.
3. **Green Supply Chain:** Reducing environmental impact by implementing sustainable practices in the supply chain.

Challenges in Implementing Supply Chain Management

- **Disruptions in the Supply Chain** → Global crises, such as a pandemic or geopolitical conflict, can disrupt the distribution of goods.
- **Market Demand Fluctuations** → Companies must have a flexible strategy to deal with sudden spikes in demand.
- **Technology Limitations** → Implementation of technology in SCM requires huge investment and adequate technical skills.

Conclusion

Supply Chain Management is a key element in implementing business strategies that ensure operational efficiency, cost reduction, and increased customer satisfaction. With the right strategy, companies can create a more resilient, flexible, and sustainable supply chain.

9.4 Technology and Innovation in Operations

Understanding Technology and Innovation in Operations

Technology and innovation in operations is the application of technological solutions to improve efficiency, productivity, and competitiveness in the production process. With the development of **Industry 4.0** , companies are increasingly adopting digital technologies to optimize supply chains and manufacturing processes.

According to **Porter (2020)** , technology integration in business operations enables companies to create added value through automation, data analysis, and artificial intelligence (AI).

Types of Technology in Operations

☑ **1. Automation and Robotics**

- The use of automated machines and robots in production to increase efficiency.
- Example: Tesla uses robots in its electric car assembly line to reduce human error and increase production speed.

☑ **2. Internet of Things (IoT) in Manufacturing**

- Connect devices in the production process for real-time monitoring and analysis.
- Example: General Electric uses IoT to automatically monitor machine performance and reduce downtime.

✓ 3. Artificial Intelligence (AI) and Big Data Analytics

- AI is used to analyze operational data and predict machine maintenance needs.
- Example: Amazon uses AI algorithms to optimize warehouse management and predict customer demand.

✓ 4. 3D Printing (Additive Manufacturing)

- Three-dimensional printing technology enables the production of prototypes and parts at lower costs.
- Example: Boeing uses 3D printing to produce aircraft components from lighter and stronger materials.

✓ 5. Blockchain in Supply Chain

- Blockchain technology is used to increase transparency and security in the supply chain.
- Example: Walmart uses blockchain to track the origin of food products to improve food safety.

Impact of Technology Innovation on Operations

1. **Increased Production Efficiency** – Automation and AI enable faster and more accurate production.
2. **Reducing Operational Costs** – Technologies such as IoT and predictive maintenance help reduce machine maintenance costs.
3. **Improved Product Quality** – Real-time data analysis enables companies

to identify and fix defects early.

4. **Speed of Response to Market** – Digital manufacturing technology enables more flexible production according to customer demand.

Challenges in Implementing Technology in Operations

- **High Initial Investment** → Implementing advanced technology requires large costs.
- **Lack of Skilled Human Resources** → Companies must train employees to operate new technologies.
- **Data Security and Privacy** → The use of IoT and AI increases the risk of industrial data leakage.

- **Conclusion**

Technology and innovation play a vital role in improving the efficiency and competitiveness of a company's operations. By implementing solutions such as automation, AI, IoT, and blockchain, companies can increase productivity, reduce costs, and improve customer satisfaction. However, challenges such as high investment and the need for skilled labor need to be overcome so that technology can be optimally implemented.

Case Study: Production Efficiency in Manufacturing Industry

Background

PT Manufaktur Prima is one of the largest manufacturing companies in Indonesia engaged in the production of household electronic devices. In recent years, the company has faced challenges in the form of increasing production costs, inefficiencies in the supply chain, and tight competition with cheaper imported products.

To overcome this challenge, PT Manufaktur Prima began implementing **Lean Manufacturing and Six Sigma strategies** to improve operational efficiency and improve product quality without significantly increasing production costs.

Challenges Faced

1. **Waste in the production process**

- High defect rate in products which causes additional cost for repair.
- Suboptimal production processes result in long waiting times and increased labor costs.

1. **Constraints in supply chain management**

- Delays in procurement of raw materials due to lack of coordination with suppliers.
- Fluctuations in raw material prices have an impact on increasing production costs.

1. **Lack of adoption of modern production technologies**

- Still relying on conventional production methods that are less efficient.
- Lack of investment in automation technologies that can increase productivity.

Strategies Implemented

1. **Lean Manufacturing Implementation**

- Eliminate non-value added activities (waste) in production.
- Adopting a **Just-In-Time (JIT) system** to optimize inventory management and reduce raw material waste.

- Implementing the **Kaizen (Continuous Improvement) principle** by involving employees in work process innovation.

1. **Implementing Six Sigma for Quality Improvement**

- Using the **DMAIC (Define, Measure, Analyze, Improve, Control) method** to identify and reduce production defects.
- Improving quality standards through employee training and the use of statistical tools in production process evaluation.

1. **Supply Chain Management Optimization**

- Establish long-term cooperation with suppliers to ensure the stability of raw material supply.
- Using **an ERP (Enterprise Resource Planning) system** to increase transparency in the supply chain.

1. **Investment in Technology and Automation**

- Adopting robotics-based production systems to increase efficiency and reduce human error.
- Using **the Internet of Things (IoT)** in real-time machine performance monitoring to prevent production downtime.

Implementation Results

After one year of implementing this strategy, PT Manufaktur Prima succeeded in:

- Reduce product defect rate by **40%** .
- Increase production efficiency by **reducing waiting times by up to 30%** .
- Reduce operational costs by up to **20%** by reducing waste of raw materials and labor.

- Increase customer satisfaction with higher quality products and more competitive prices.

Student Assignment

As an operations management consultant, you are asked to analyze the success of PT Manufaktur Prima's strategy and provide additional recommendations to improve production efficiency. Answer the following questions:

1. **Implementation Success Analysis**

- What factors are the key to PT Manufaktur Prima's success in increasing its production efficiency?
- How do Lean Manufacturing and Six Sigma contribute to reducing production costs and improving quality?

1. **Production Optimization Strategy**

- What additional steps can the company take to further improve production efficiency?
- How can the latest technologies such as **AI and blockchain** be applied in PT Manufaktur Prima's supply chain management?

1. **Risk Evaluation in Strategy Implementation**

- What are the biggest challenges in implementing Lean Manufacturing and Six Sigma strategies in manufacturing companies?
- How to overcome employee resistance to changes in production processes?

1. **Future Strategy Recommendations**

- If you were the Chief Operating Officer (COO) at PT Manufaktur Prima, what strategies would you implement to maintain the company's competitive advantage?

- How can companies ensure continuity of innovation in their production operations?

Expected Output:

- Production efficiency strategy analysis report of PT Manufaktur Prima.
- Recommendations for innovation in operating and production systems.
- A short presentation on strategic solutions for PT Manufaktur Prima.

CHAPTER 10: Strategy Implementation – Financial Management and Accounting

10.1 The Role of Finance in Strategy Implementation

Understanding the Role of Finance in Strategic Management

Financial management plays a very important role in implementing a company's strategy. The right financial decisions can determine the success of a business strategy, both in terms of expansion, operational efficiency, and company sustainability.

According to **Brigham & Houston (2021)** , good financial management allows companies to allocate resources optimally, manage risks, and increase long-term profitability.

The Role of Finance in Strategy Implementation

✔ **1. Financial Planning and Resource Allocation**

- Develop a strategic budget that supports short-term and long-term business goals.
- Example: Retail companies such as Indomaret use expansion budgets to strategically increase the number of outlets.

✅ 2. Cash Flow Management

- Ensuring the company has sufficient liquidity to carry out operations and investments.
- Example: Unilever Indonesia manages cash flow with a structured payment system to avoid liquidity problems.

✅ 3. Capital Structure Optimization

- Determining the right combination of equity and debt to fund business strategy.
- Example: Startup companies use financing from investors (venture capital) to support business growth.

✅ 4. Cost Control and Operational Efficiency

- Reduce operational costs without sacrificing product and service quality.
- Example: Apple implements a cost management strategy with efficiency in its global supply chain.

✅ 5. Financial Performance Measurement

- Using financial ratios such as **ROA (Return on Assets), ROE (Return on Equity), and EBITDA (Earnings Before Interest, Taxes, Depreciation, and Amortization)** to evaluate the success of a business strategy.
- Example: Bank BCA routinely analyzes its financial ratios to maintain profitability and competitiveness.

The Relationship between Financial Management and Competitive Advantage

- **Companies with a solid financial strategy can be more flexible in the face of economic uncertainty.**
- **The right investment decisions enable companies to stay innovative and grow.**
- **Efficient financial management can increase shareholder value and strengthen the company's image in the eyes of investors.**

Conclusion

Finance plays a key role in implementing business strategies. With effective financial management, companies can allocate resources optimally, manage risks, and achieve sustainable growth.

10.2 Financial Statement Analysis for Strategic Decision Making

Understanding Financial Report Analysis

Financial statement analysis is the process of evaluating a company's financial performance based on historical data contained in the financial statements. This process aims to understand the company's financial condition, identify financial trends, and provide a basis for strategic decision making.

According to **Fraser & Ormiston (2020)** , financial report analysis helps stakeholders evaluate the company's financial health and direct more appropriate strategic policies.

Main Components in Financial Reports

✓ 1. Income Statement

- Measuring a company's financial performance in a certain period based

on revenue, costs, and net profit.
- Example: PT XYZ recorded a 20% increase in net profit in 2023 compared to the previous year.

✓ 2. Financial Balance Sheet

- Provides an overview of a company's assets, liabilities, and equity at a point in time.
- Example: Companies with low debt ratios have greater financial flexibility.

✓ 3. Cash Flow Statement

- Identifying how a company manages cash inflows and outflows, as well as its liquidity.
- Example: Positive cash flow from operations indicates that the business is able to fund operations without relying on borrowing.

✓ 4. Statement of Changes in Equity

- Shows the change in shareholders' equity over a period of time.
- Example: Companies that frequently pay dividends demonstrate a strategy of returning value to shareholders.

Financial Statement Analysis Methods

✓ 1. Financial Ratio Analysis

- Using financial ratios to assess a company's profitability, liquidity, and solvency.
- Example:
- **Liquidity Ratio:** Current Ratio = Current Assets / Current Liabilities.
- **Profitability Ratio:** Return on Assets (ROA) = Net Profit / Total Assets.

- **Solvency Ratio:** Debt to Equity Ratio (DER) = Total Debt / Equity.

✔ 2. Trend Analysis

- Comparing a company's financial performance over several periods to identify patterns of growth or decline.
- Example: If revenue increases consistently every year, then the company is in a positive growth trend.

✔ 3. Benchmarking Analysis

- Comparing a company's financial statements with competitors or industry standards.
- Example: If a company's profit margin is higher than its competitors, then its business strategy is more effective.

✔ 4. Common Size Analysis

- Presenting financial reports in percentage form to understand cost structure and revenue sources.
- Example: If operating costs reach 60% of total revenue, then the company needs to control operating costs to be more efficient.

The Role of Financial Statement Analysis in Strategic Decision Making

- **Determining investment strategies** – Financial reports help companies allocate funds to profitable projects.
- **Managing financial risk** – By understanding capital structure and financial ratios, companies can reduce reliance on excessive debt.
- **Assisting in business expansion** – Financial data is used to assess the feasibility of expansion and measure its impact on cash flow.
- **Improve operational efficiency** – Cost and profit margin analysis helps companies optimize operations.

Conclusion

Financial statement analysis is an essential tool in strategic decision-making that enables companies to assess financial performance, manage risk, and design sustainable growth strategies. By using analytical techniques such as financial ratios, trends, and benchmarking, management can ensure that business decisions are based on accurate and relevant data.

10.3 Financial Risk Management

Understanding Financial Risk Management

Financial risk management is the process of identifying, analyzing, and mitigating potential risks that may affect a company's financial stability. Financial risks can arise from a variety of factors, including market volatility, interest rate changes, exchange rate fluctuations, and credit risk.

According to **Rejda & McNamara (2021)** , financial risk management aims to protect company assets, maintain liquidity, and ensure business continuity in uncertain economic conditions.

Types of Financial Risk in Business Strategy

✓ **1. Market Risk (Market Risk)**

- Risks arising from changes in market prices, such as fluctuations in stock prices, commodities, or currency exchange rates.
- Example: Export companies are negatively impacted when the rupiah exchange rate weakens against the US dollar.

✓ **2. Credit Risk (Credit Risk)**

- The risk of default by customers or business partners on their financial obligations.
- Example: Banks are at risk if customers are unable to repay their loans on schedule.

✓ 3. Liquidity Risk

- The company's inability to meet short-term obligations due to limited cash flow.
- Example: A company that has large assets but has difficulty paying operational obligations.

✓ 4. Operational Risk

- Risks arising from failures in business processes, human error, or external factors.
- Example: Disruptions in information technology systems cause financial transactions to be disrupted.

✓ 5. Legal and Regulatory Risk

- Changes in government policy or regulations that may affect the company's financial condition.
- Example: Implementation of new taxes that increase the company's cost burden.

Financial Risk Management Strategy

✓ 1. Diversify Investment Portfolio

- Spreading investments across multiple assets to reduce the impact of market risk.

- Example: Companies that have assets in the form of stocks, bonds and property can reduce exposure to stock market fluctuations.

✅ 2. Hedging against Market Risk

- Using financial instruments such as futures or options to reduce exchange rate and interest rate risks.
- Example: An export company uses a hedging contract to protect against currency exchange rates.

✅ 3. Effective Liquidity Management

- Optimize cash management and estimate funding needs to avoid liquidity risks.
- Example: The company sets a minimum cash reserve policy to deal with emergencies.

✅ 4. Credit Evaluation and Receivables Management

- Analyze customer credibility before granting credit to reduce the risk of default.
- Example: Banks implement a credit scoring system before providing loans to customers.

✅ 5. Compliance with Financial Regulations and Policies

- Ensure compliance with financial and legal standards to avoid legal risks.
- Example: Companies that comply with tax regulations can avoid sanctions and fines.

The Importance of Financial Risk Management in Strategy Implementation

- **Maintaining Financial Stability** – Avoiding operational disruptions due to financial instability.
- **Increasing Investor Confidence** – Investors have more confidence in companies that have good financial risk management.
- **Supporting Strategic Decisions** – Well-managed risks enable companies to make business decisions with more confidence.
- **Reducing Uncertainty** – An effective risk strategy helps companies face economic and financial challenges with better preparedness.

Conclusion

Financial risk management is an important aspect of business strategy that ensures the sustainability and stability of a company. By implementing appropriate risk mitigation strategies, companies can avoid major losses, improve financial efficiency, and strengthen competitiveness in the industry.

10.4 Strategic Investments in the Company

Understanding Strategic Investment

Strategic investment is an investment decision made by a company to support long-term growth, increase competitiveness, and create added value for shareholders. This investment involves allocating resources to projects that can provide sustainable benefits.

According to **Bodie, Kane, & Marcus (2020)** , strategic investment aims to strengthen the company's market position, increase operational efficiency, and take advantage of innovation and technology opportunities.

Types of Strategic Investments

✔ 1. Investment in Physical Assets

- Includes the purchase of equipment, factories, or infrastructure that supports production.
- Example: Tesla is building a gigafactory to increase its electric car battery production capacity.

✔ 2. Investment in Technology Development

- Focus on research and development (R&D) to create product and service innovations.
- Example: Google is investing billions of dollars in the development of artificial intelligence (AI).

✔ 3. Investment in Market Expansion

- Entering new markets through geographic expansion or new customer segments.
- Example: Starbucks opens stores in developing countries to expand its global customer base.

✔ 4. Investment in Acquisitions and Mergers

- Acquiring other companies to strengthen business synergies and portfolio diversification.
- Example: Facebook acquired WhatsApp to expand its dominance in the digital communications sector.

✔ 5. Investment in Human Resources

- Conducting HR training and development to improve workforce capabilities and competitiveness.

- Example: Technology companies like Microsoft offer digital certification programs for their employees.

Strategy in Strategic Investment

✓ 1. Capital Budgeting

- Using methods such as **Net Present Value (NPV), Internal Rate of Return (IRR), and Payback Period** to assess the feasibility of an investment.
- Example: Companies use NPV analysis to determine whether an investment project will provide future benefits.

✓ 2. Diversify Investment Portfolio

- Allocating funds to different sectors or products to reduce investment risk.
- Example: Samsung not only invests in electronics, but also in the semiconductor and medical equipment industries.

✓ 3. Strategic Partnerships and Joint Ventures

- Establish partnerships with other companies to expand business reach without making large investments.
- Example: Toyota and Panasonic are collaborating on the development of electric vehicle batteries.

✓ 4. Investment Risk Evaluation

- Analyze risk factors such as economic uncertainty, regulatory changes, and market volatility before investing.
- Example: A company conducts due diligence before acquiring a new business.

The Importance of Strategic Investment in Corporate Sustainability

- **Strengthening market position** – Companies that invest in innovation and expansion have higher competitiveness.
- **Improving operational efficiency** – Investments in technology and infrastructure can increase productivity.
- **Increasing shareholder value** – The right investment decisions can increase a company's profits and share price.
- **Adapting to industry changes** – Investing in new trends, such as digitalization and renewable energy, ensures companies stay relevant.

Conclusion

Strategic investment is an important part of implementing a business strategy that allows a company to grow and remain competitive in the long term. By conducting proper financial analysis and managing investment risks, companies can ensure that the resources allocated provide optimal results.

Case Study: Financial Management in Business Expansion

Background

PT Global Retail is one of the largest retail companies in Indonesia with hundreds of outlets in various cities. Along with changes in consumer behavior that are increasingly shifting to e-commerce platforms, PT Global Retail faces challenges to stay relevant and competitive in the market. To maintain its position, the company decided to expand its business into the digital segment by launching its own e-commerce platform.

However, this expansion requires significant investment in technology development, digital marketing, and more efficient supply chain management. Therefore, companies need to ensure that their financial strategies can support these investments without compromising the company's financial stability.

Challenges Faced

1. **Funding for Digital Expansion**

- Companies need large capital to develop e-commerce platforms and expand logistics networks.
- Have to choose between funding through debt, equity, or strategic partnerships.

1. **Financial Risk Management**

- Managing cash flow to remain liquid during the expansion process.
- Anticipating the risk of investment failure due to digital market uncertainty.

1. **Investment Profitability Analysis**

- Determining whether investing in e-commerce will provide long-term benefits.
- Using **the Net Present Value (NPV)** and **Internal Rate of Return (IRR) methods** to evaluate project feasibility.

1. **Capital Structure Management**

- Maintain a balance between the use of equity and loans so as not to increase

excessive financial risk.
- Ensuring that the debt to equity ratio remains healthy.

Financial Strategies Implemented

1. **Optimal Use of Funding Sources**

- PT Global Retail issued corporate bonds to obtain expansion funds without reducing equity ownership.
- Collaborate with strategic investors to obtain additional funding.

1. **Effective Cash Flow Management**

- Using the **Cash Flow Forecasting system** to ensure the availability of operational funds during the expansion process.
- Delaying non-essential investments to allocate more funds to digital infrastructure.

1. **Implementation of Financial Risk Management**

- Using **hedging strategies** to reduce exchange rate risk as most of the technology infrastructure is imported.
- Analyze the market scenario before going for full expansion.

1. **Sustainable Investment Evaluation**

- Periodically review the performance of the e-commerce platform using financial indicators such as **Return on Investment (ROI)** and **Gross Margin** .
- Optimizing digital marketing strategies based on customer data analysis results.

Implementation Results

After one year of implementation, PT Global Retail succeeded in:

- Increase revenue from e-commerce channels up to **35%** of total revenue.
- Optimizing cash flow with **a 20% reduction in operating costs** through supply chain automation.
- Maintaining **the debt-to-equity ratio below 1.5** ensures the company's financial stability.

Student Assignment

As a financial analyst, you are asked to evaluate the success of PT Global Retail's financial strategy and provide additional recommendations to improve the effectiveness of business expansion. Answer the following questions:

1. **Evaluation of Implementation Success**

- What factors are key to PT Global Retail's success in its digital expansion?
- How does the funding strategy used help in supporting this expansion?

1. **Financial Optimization Strategy**

- What steps can be taken to increase the profitability of investments in e-commerce platforms?
- How can companies reduce further financial risks during their business expansion?

1. **Financial Risk Analysis**

- What is the biggest challenge in maintaining a balance between investment and liquidity?
- How can financial risk management strategies be implemented to ensure

business sustainability?

1. **Future Strategy Recommendations**

- If you were the Chief Financial Officer (CFO) at PT Global Retail, what financial strategies would you implement to maintain the company's growth?
- How can companies continue to innovate in financial management to support expansion into the digital sector?

Expected Output:

- Financial strategy analysis report of PT Global Retail.
- Financial strategy recommendations to increase profitability and mitigate risk.
- A short presentation on strategic solutions for PT Global Retail.

CHAPTER 11: Strategy Implementation – Information Systems and Technology

11.1 Digitalization and Business Transformation

Understanding Digitalization and Business Transformation

Digitalization is the process of transforming traditional business models into digital-based ones to improve efficiency, competitiveness, and innovation. Business transformation through digitalization enables companies to adapt to market changes and create new value for customers.

According to **Westerman, Bonnet, & McAfee (2021)**, digital transformation is not just about adopting new technologies, but also changing organizational culture, business processes, and company strategies to be more adaptive and responsive to market changes.

Components of Digitalization in Business

✓ 1. Business Process Automation

- Using digital systems to reduce manual work and increase operational efficiency.
- Example: Manufacturing companies adopt **robotics** to speed up produc-

tion processes.

✓ 2. Cloud Computing and Digital Infrastructure

- Migrating to cloud-based services allows for more flexible and efficient data access.
- Example: An e-commerce company uses **Amazon Web Services (AWS)** for hosting and data analysis.

✓ 3. Digital Marketing and Customer Engagement

- Using digital platforms to understand customer behavior and increase engagement.
- Example: Netflix uses customer data analysis to recommend relevant content.

✓ 4. E-Commerce and Digital Platforms

- Leveraging digital channels to sell products and services more widely.
- Example: Tokopedia and Shopee are changing the way consumers shop in Indonesia.

✓ 5. Data Analytics and Decision-Making

- Using **Big Data** and **Artificial Intelligence (AI)** to improve strategic decision making.
- Example: Banks use data analysis to detect potential fraud in financial transactions.

The Advantages of Digital Transformation in Business Strategy

- **Improve Operational Efficiency** – Process automation reduces costs and increases productivity.
- **Improving Customer Experience** – Technology enables more personal and responsive service.
- **Increasing Competitiveness** – Companies that implement digitalization are more adaptive to market changes.
- **Supporting Product and Service Innovation** – Customer data can be used to create products that better suit market needs.

Challenges in Implementing Digitalization

- **Expensive Technology Investments** → Companies must consider ROI before adopting digital systems.
- **Resistance to Change** → Employees and management may have difficulty adapting to new technologies.
- **Data Security and Privacy** → Increasing cyber threats require a strong security system.
- **Digital Skills Gap** → Companies must train employees to have relevant digital skills.

Conclusion

Digital transformation is a strategic step for companies to survive and thrive in the digital era. By adopting technologies such as **AI, Big Data, Cloud Computing, and E-Commerce**, companies can improve operational efficiency, create better customer experiences, and ensure long-term competitiveness.

11.2 The Role of Big Data and AI in Strategic Management

Understanding Big Data and Artificial Intelligence (AI)

Big Data is a collection of large amounts of data collected from various sources and analyzed to produce useful insights for business decision making. Meanwhile, **Artificial Intelligence (AI)** is a technology that allows systems to learn, analyze, and make decisions automatically without human intervention.

According to **McKinsey & Company (2021)** , the combination of Big Data and AI can improve operational efficiency, personalize customer service, and help companies create more accurate data-based business strategies.

The Role of Big Data and AI in Strategy Management

☑ **1. Data-Driven Decision Making**

- Big Data enables more accurate analysis of market trends.
- Example: Retail companies like Walmart use Big Data analytics to optimize inventory based on customer purchasing patterns.

☑ **2. Predict Market Trends and Demand**

- AI can analyze historical data to predict future customer demand.
- Example: Amazon uses AI to personalize product recommendations based on customer shopping behavior.

☑ **3. Operational Optimization and Business Efficiency**

- AI can automate routine tasks, increasing productivity and efficiency.
- Example: Google uses AI in its data centers to optimize energy consumption and reduce operational costs.

☑ **4. Improve Customer Experience**

- AI enables chatbots and virtual assistants to provide faster and more accurate customer service.
- Example: Banks like BCA use AI-based chatbots to answer customer questions automatically.

✅ **5. Risk Management and Fraud Detection**

- Big Data and AI can detect suspicious transaction patterns in the financial system.
- Example: Bank Indonesia applies AI in its financial transaction monitoring system to reduce the risk of money laundering.

The Benefits of Using Big Data and AI in Business Strategy

- **Faster and more accurate decisions** – AI can analyze data in seconds and provide data-driven recommendations.
- **Increased operational efficiency** – AI-based automation reduces reliance on time-consuming manual processes.
- **Competitive advantage** – Companies that adopt AI and Big Data can be more responsive to market changes.
- **Personalization of customer service** – Data analytics enables customer experiences that are more tailored to individual preferences.

Challenges in Implementing Big Data and AI

- **Huge technology investment** → AI implementation requires robust infrastructure and expensive resources.
- **Skilled workforce shortage** → Companies need AI specialists and data scientists to manage these systems.

- **Data security and privacy** → Big Data contains sensitive information that must be protected from cyber threats.
- **System integration complexity** → Integrating AI with existing systems often requires major adaptations.

Conclusion

Big Data and AI play a vital role in strategic management by increasing efficiency, accelerating decision-making, and enhancing customer experience. Companies that are able to integrate these technologies well will have a significant competitive advantage in the digital era.

11.3 IT Security Strategy and Risk Management

Understanding IT Security and Risk Management

Information technology security (IT Security) is a set of practices and systems designed to protect data, systems, and networks from cyber threats. IT risk management includes the identification, analysis, and mitigation of technology-related risks within an organization.

According to **ISO/IEC 27001**, IT risk management focuses on implementing information security controls to protect an organization's data from threats such as cyberattacks, data leaks, and system failures.

Types of IT Security Threats in Strategy Management

✅ 1. Cyber Attacks

- Including hacking, malware, ransomware, and DDoS attacks that can cripple a company's systems.
- Example: A ransomware attack on a multinational company results in

data being encrypted and can only be accessed again by paying the ransom.

✓ 2. Data Breach

- Occurs when a company's sensitive data is stolen or accessed without permission.
- Example: An e-commerce company experiences customer data theft which results in a loss of customer trust.

✓ 3. Insider Threat (Threat from Within)

- Threats originating from employees or business partners who abuse access to company systems.
- Example: An employee dissatisfied with the company leaks confidential information to a competitor.

✓ 4. IT System Failure and Downtime

- Disruptions to servers or IT systems that can hinder business operations.
- Example: An online payment system failure resulted in lost transactions for several hours.

✓ 5. Compliance with Regulations and Data Privacy

- Companies must ensure that their IT systems comply with regulations such as **GDPR, ISO 27001, and the Data Protection Act** .
- Example: Companies that do not comply with data protection regulations may be subject to large fines by the relevant authorities.

IT Security Strategy and Risk Management

✔ 1. Implementation of Layered Security System

- Using firewalls, encryption, multi-factor authentication (MFA), and intrusion detection systems (IDS) to protect systems from cyber threats.

✔ 2. Identity Access Management (IAM)

- Restrict access to sensitive data to authorized parties only.
- Example: A company implements a **Role-Based Access Control (RBAC) policy** so that only certain employees can access important data.

✔ 3. Cyber Security Training and Awareness for Employees

- Educate employees about cybersecurity practices, such as recognizing phishing and using strong passwords.

✔ 4. Use of AI and Machine Learning Technology for IT Security

- AI can be used to detect suspicious patterns and prevent cyber attacks automatically.
- Example: Banks use AI to detect suspicious transactions and stop potentially fraudulent activities.

✔ 5. Framework-Based IT Risk Management

- Using standards such as **the NIST Cybersecurity Framework** or **COBIT** to manage IT risks more effectively.

✔ 6. Disaster Recovery Plan

- Develop strategies to ensure business operations can recover quickly after a cyber attack or system disruption.
- Example: A company has **cloud-based data backups** that can be accessed again within minutes after the primary system fails.

Benefits of Implementing IT Security in Business Strategy

- **Reduce the risk of data loss** → Companies can protect their digital assets with a strong security system.
- **Maintaining customer reputation and trust** → Good data protection increases customer loyalty.
- **Ensuring regulatory compliance** → Avoiding legal sanctions due to data protection violations.
- **Improving business resilience** → Companies can continue operating despite cyber threats.

Challenges in IT Risk Management

- **The development of increasingly complex cyber threats** → Companies must always update their security systems.
- **Budget constraints for IT security** → Not all companies have sufficient funds to implement maximum protection.
- **Lack of employee awareness and compliance** → Human error is still a major factor in data leaks.
- **Integration of security systems with existing technologies** → Implementation of new security technologies must be compatible with existing systems.

Conclusion

IT security and risk management strategies are critical elements of business continuity in the digital age. By implementing robust security systems, properly managing IT risks, and increasing security awareness across the organization, companies can protect their digital assets and ensure the continuity of their operations.

11.4 ERP Implementation in Corporate Strategy

Understanding ERP (Enterprise Resource Planning)

ERP (Enterprise Resource Planning) is an integrated system that manages various aspects of a business such as finance, production, marketing, human resources, and supply chain in one technology-based platform. ERP helps companies improve efficiency, transparency, and data-based decision making.

According to **Monk & Wagner (2020)**, ERP implementation allows companies to optimize business processes, reduce data redundancy, and improve collaboration between departments.

Main Functions of ERP in Business Strategy

☑ **1. Data and Business Process Integration**

- ERP allows different departments to share data in one centralized system.
- Example: SAP ERP is used by multinational companies to integrate financial, production, and distribution management in one platform.

☑ **2. Increased Operational Efficiency**

- Automation of various business processes such as inventory management, payments, and financial reporting.
- Example: Retail companies such as Indomaret use ERP to manage stock of goods across all its branches in real-time.

✓ 3. More Accurate Decision Making

- ERP provides dashboards and analytical reports to support data-driven decision making.
- Example: Banks use ERP to analyze financial trends and minimize credit risk.

✓ 4. More Effective Supply Chain Management

- ERP allows for more coordinated production and distribution planning.
- Example: Toyota uses ERP to optimize its supply chain and reduce waste in production.

✓ 5. Increased Compliance with Regulations

- ERP helps companies ensure compliance with applicable accounting, taxation and legal standards.
- Example: A pharmaceutical company uses ERP to comply with regulations in the production and distribution of drugs.

ERP Implementation Strategy in Companies

✓ 1. Selecting the Right ERP System

- Choosing an ERP solution that fits your company's size, needs, and industry.
- Example: Manufacturing companies are more suited to using **SAP ERP** , while small-scale companies can choose **Odoo ERP** .

✓ 2. Change Management and Employee Training

- Conduct training so that employees can adopt the ERP system easily.

- Example: The company conducted ERP training for the finance and operations teams before the system was fully implemented.

✓ 3. Effective Data Migration

- Ensuring data from legacy systems can be transferred to the ERP system without losing critical information.
- Example: A company conducts a data migration trial before full ERP implementation to avoid technical errors.

✓ 4. Continuous Evaluation and Optimization

- After implementation, companies must continuously evaluate ERP performance to improve efficiency.
- Example: The company's IT team periodically audits the ERP system to ensure its functionality remains optimal.

Challenges in ERP Implementation

- **High Implementation Costs** → ERP requires huge investments in software, training, and maintenance.
- **Resistance to Change** → Employees are often reluctant to adapt to new systems.
- **Integration Complexity** → ERP must be able to integrate with existing systems without disrupting operations.
- **Data Security and Privacy** → Since ERP manages a lot of sensitive data, security risks need to be taken seriously.

Conclusion

Implementing ERP in a company's strategy is an important step in improving operational efficiency, transparency, and effectiveness. With careful planning, adequate training, and continuous evaluation, companies can optimize the use of ERP to achieve competitive advantage.

Case Study: Digital Transformation in a Retail Company

Background

PT Retail Digital Indonesia is one of the largest retail companies in Indonesia with a network of physical stores across the country. However, with the increasing adoption of e-commerce and changes in consumer behavior that prefer online shopping, the company faces major challenges in maintaining its competitiveness.

To face this challenge, PT Retail Digital Indonesia decided to carry out a complete digital transformation. This step includes e-commerce integration, ERP system implementation, utilization of Big Data and AI for customer analysis, and implementation of cybersecurity strategies.

Challenges Faced

1. **Changes in Consumer Behavior**

- Consumers prefer to shop online rather than visit physical stores.
- Increasing demand for more personal and efficient shopping experiences.

1. **Competition with E-Commerce Platforms**

- Competitors like Shopee and Tokopedia offer an easier shopping experience and competitive prices.
- The difficulty in building competitive advantage in the digital market.

1. **Technology Integration into Business Operations**

- Migrating from traditional to digital systems requires significant investment and employee training.
- Risks in managing customer data security and online transactions.

Implemented Digital Transformation Strategy

1. **Developing Your Own E-Commerce Platform**

- Building an online shopping platform integrated with physical stores.
- Offering digital payment features, fast delivery, and AI chatbot-based customer service.

1. **ERP System Implementation**

- Using ERP to integrate stock management, logistics and finance in one system.
- Optimizing the supply chain process to be more efficient and responsive to market demand.

1. **Utilization of Big Data and AI**

- Using customer data analytics to personalize product recommendations.
- AI is used in chatbot systems to improve customer service automatically.

1. **Enhanced Cyber Security and IT Risk Management**

- Using data encryption and multi-factor authentication systems to protect customer information.
- Implementing an **ISO 27001 -based security framework** and applicable data protection regulations.

Implementation Results

- **Increased online sales by 40% in the first year.**
- **Reduction of operational costs by 25% through automation of business processes with ERP.**
- **Increasing customer loyalty by implementing customer data-based reward programs.**
- **Reducing cybersecurity risks through implementing tighter security systems.**

Student Assignment

As a digital strategy management consultant, you are asked to evaluate the success of the digital transformation strategy implemented by PT Retail Digital Indonesia and provide additional recommendations to improve the effectiveness of the strategy. Answer the following questions:

1. **Evaluation of Implementation Success**

- What factors contributed to the success of PT Retail Digital Indonesia's digital transformation?
- How does ERP implementation impact a company's operational efficiency?

1. **Optimizing Digitalization Strategy**

- What additional steps can be taken to improve a company's competitiveness in the digital retail industry?
- How can companies better leverage AI to improve customer experience?

1. **IT Security Analysis and Risk Management**

- What are the main challenges in keeping customer data secure in the e-commerce ecosystem?

- What strategies can be implemented to improve the security of digital transactions?

1. **Future Strategy Recommendations**

- If you were the Chief Digital Officer (CDO) of PT Retail Digital Indonesia, what strategies would you implement to maintain the company's digital growth?
- How can companies integrate technological innovations such as blockchain into supply chain management?

Expected Output:

- Digital transformation strategy analysis report of PT Retail Digital Indonesia.
- Recommendations for digitalization strategies to improve company competitiveness.
- A short presentation on strategic solutions for PT Retail Digital Indonesia.

CHAPTER 12: Strategy Evaluation and Control

12.1 The Concept of Evaluation and Control in Strategic Management

Understanding Strategy Evaluation and Control

Strategy evaluation and control is a systematic process to assess the effectiveness of implemented business strategies, identify performance gaps, and make necessary improvements so that organizational goals can be achieved optimally.

According to **David (2020)** , strategy evaluation aims to ensure that the implemented strategy remains relevant to market conditions, the business environment, and organizational goals.

Objectives of Strategy Evaluation and Control

✓ 1. Measuring Strategy Performance

- Assess whether the results achieved are in accordance with the targets that have been set.
- Example: A manufacturing company evaluates production efficiency based on increased output and reduced operating costs.

✓ 2. Adapting Strategy to Business Environment

- Review whether external changes such as regulations, industry trends, or competition require strategy adjustments.
- Example: An e-commerce company evaluates changes in digital tax policies and adjusts its pricing strategy.

✓ 3. Identifying Causes of Strategy Failure

- Finding internal or external factors that cause strategies not to go according to plan.
- Example: Failed business expansion due to lack of proper market research before entering a new territory.

✓ 4. Increase Efficiency and Effectiveness

- Optimizing resource utilization and correcting weaknesses in strategy implementation.
- Example: A retail company evaluates the effectiveness of their digital marketing strategy through sales conversion metrics.

Stages of Strategy Evaluation and Control

1. Setting Performance Standards

- Determine the parameters that will be used to assess the success of the strategy, such as profitability, market growth, or customer satisfaction.

1. Measuring Actual Performance

- Compare actual results with established standards to identify performance gaps.

1. **Analyzing Deviations**

- Identify the root causes of differences between expected and achieved results.

1. **Taking Corrective Action**

- Make strategic improvements or adjust operational tactics based on evaluation results.

Strategy Evaluation and Control Methods

✓ 1. Quantitative Performance Measurement

- Using financial and operational indicators such as **Return on Investment (ROI), Net Profit Margin, and Market Share** .

✓ 2. Qualitative Evaluation

- Assess strategy effectiveness based on customer perceptions, organizational culture, and employee satisfaction.

✓ 3. Strategy Audit

- The process of systematically reviewing all elements of a strategy, including objectives, implementation, and results.

Conclusion

Strategy evaluation and control is an important aspect of strategic management that ensures that the organization remains on track towards achieving its goals. By conducting regular evaluations, companies can adjust their strategies to changing business conditions and optimize their performance.

12.2 Balanced Scorecard as an Evaluation Tool

Understanding Balanced Scorecard (BSC)

Balanced Scorecard (BSC) is a strategic management tool used to measure and evaluate organizational performance from multiple perspectives. BSC was developed by **Kaplan and Norton (1992)** and helps companies translate vision and strategy into measurable actions.

BSC focuses not only on financial aspects, but also on other indicators that reflect the overall health and sustainability of the business.

Four Perspectives in the Balanced Scorecard

✓ 1. Financial Perspective

- Measuring the success of strategies in increasing profitability and shareholder value.
- Main indicators: **Return on Investment (ROI), Net Profit Margin, Cash Flow, Revenue Growth** .
- Example: A manufacturing company evaluates the effectiveness of its pricing strategy by looking at the profit margin it achieves.

✅ 2. Customer Perspective

- Assess the extent to which the company is able to meet customer needs and increase their loyalty.
- Main indicators: **Customer Satisfaction Index, Retention Rate, Market Share, Net Promoter Score (NPS)** .
- Example: An e-commerce company evaluates its customer service strategy based on customer satisfaction levels.

✅ 3. Internal Business Process Perspective

- Measuring operational efficiency and innovation in production or service processes.
- Main indicators: **Lead Time, Product Defect Rate, Process Efficiency, Supply Chain Optimization** .
- Example: A manufacturing company uses BSC to evaluate the effectiveness of lean manufacturing strategies in reducing waste.

✅ 4. Learning and Growth Perspective

- Measuring the company's ability to improve human resources and technology capabilities.
- Main indicators: **Employee Productivity, Training Hours per Employee, Innovation Rate, Employee Satisfaction** .
- Example: A technology company assesses the effectiveness of employee training programs to improve their digital skills.

Advantages of the Balanced Scorecard as an Evaluation Tool

- **Integrating financial and non-financial perspectives** → Ensuring balance in performance measurement.
- **Increase transparency and accountability** → Each business unit has responsibility in achieving targets.

- **Driving continuous improvement** → BSC provides a comprehensive overview of the effectiveness of business strategies.
- **Assisting in long-term strategic planning** → Connecting the company vision with measurable performance indicators.

Challenges in Balanced Scorecard Implementation

- **Difficulty in establishing relevant indicators** → Not all organizations have metric standards that are in line with their strategic objectives.
- **Lack of understanding and commitment from management** → BSC implementation requires full support from all levels of the organization.
- **Limitations in measuring qualitative data** → Some aspects such as innovation and work culture are difficult to measure objectively.

Conclusion

Balanced Scorecard is a strategic evaluation tool that helps companies measure and improve performance from multiple perspectives. With proper implementation, BSC can be a strong foundation for strategic decision making and achieving competitive advantage.

12.3 Strategic Risk Management

Understanding Strategic Risk Management

Strategic risk management is the process of identifying, analyzing, and mitigating risks that can affect the achievement of a company's strategic goals. These risks can originate from internal or external factors that impact business sustainability.

According to **Hill et al. (2021)** , strategic risk management helps companies anticipate challenges and develop mitigation strategies to maintain competitive advantage.

Types of Strategic Risk in a Company

✓ 1. Competitive Risk

- Intense competition can threaten a company's market position.
- Example: Retail companies face competition from e-commerce that offers lower prices and a more convenient shopping experience.

✓ 2. Regulatory and Legal Risks

- Changes in government policy or regulation may impact business operations.
- Example: Fintech companies must adapt to new regulations regarding customer data protection.

✓ 3. Economic and Market Risks

- Factors such as inflation, recession, and exchange rate fluctuations can affect business stability.
- Example: The global financial crisis impacted consumer purchasing power and business investment.

✓ 4. Technology and Innovation Risks

- Inability to adapt to technological developments can cause companies to be left behind.
- Example: Telecommunications companies that do not innovate in digital

services lose customers to more innovative competitors.

✅ 5. Operational Risk

- Disruptions in production processes, supply chains, or management errors can hamper a company's operations.
- Example: A failure in an ERP system causes disruption in a manufacturing company's inventory management.

Strategic Risk Management Strategy

✅ 1. Risk Identification and Analysis

- **SWOT Analysis, PESTEL Analysis** , or **Risk Mapping** methods to identify potential risks.

✅ 2. Risk Mitigation with Diversification

- Develop a diversified business portfolio to reduce dependence on one sector.
- Example: Energy companies invest in renewable energy sources to reduce regulatory risks on fossil fuels.

✅ 3. Application of Technology in Risk Management

- Using **Artificial Intelligence (AI)** to analyze risk trends and support decision making.
- Example: Banks use machine learning to detect potential fraud in financial transactions.

✅ 4. Financial Risk Management

- Using **hedging strategies** , financial reserves, and financial planning to deal with market uncertainty.

✓ **5. Periodic Evaluation and Adjustment of Strategy**

- Conduct regular risk audits to align business strategies with market dynamics.

Conclusion

Strategic risk management is an essential element in maintaining the sustainability and competitiveness of a company. By proactively identifying and managing risks, companies can face challenges with better preparedness and maintain business stability and growth.

12.4 Strategy Success Evaluation Study

Understanding Strategy Success Evaluation

Strategy success evaluation is a comprehensive review process of the effectiveness of strategies that have been implemented in achieving business goals. This evaluation includes performance measurements based on established indicators and analysis of the success and failure factors of the strategy.

According to **Pearce & Robinson (2020)** , strategy evaluation helps companies adjust their business direction to changes in the external and internal environment in order to remain competitive.

Strategy Success Indicators

✓ 1. Financial Performance

- Using financial metrics such as **Return on Investment (ROI), Net Profit Margin, Gross Profit Margin, and Revenue Growth** .
- Example: A technology company evaluates the success of global expansion based on increased revenue from international markets.

✓ 2. Customer Satisfaction and Loyalty

- Measuring customer satisfaction levels through **Customer Satisfaction Index (CSI), Net Promoter Score (NPS), and Retention Rate** .
- Example: A retail company uses customer satisfaction surveys to assess the effectiveness of its marketing and customer service strategies.

✓ 3. Operational Efficiency

- See how implemented strategies affect productivity and operational costs.
- Example: A manufacturing company evaluates a lean manufacturing strategy based on reducing raw material waste.

✓ 4. Increased Competitiveness

- Assess the company's position in the market compared to competitors through **Market Share Analysis and Competitive Benchmarking** .
- Example: An automotive company judges the success of a differentiation strategy based on the market share gained from their new products.

✓ 5. Adaptation to Market Changes

- Analyze the extent to which the company can respond to market and technological dynamics.

- Example: An e-commerce company evaluates the flexibility of their digital strategy in the face of changing online shopping trends.

Strategy Success Evaluation Methods

✓ 1. Gap Analysis

- Comparing actual performance with established targets.
- Example: If the annual growth target is 10% but the realization is only 7%, then it is necessary to analyze the causes of the gap.

✓ 2. Benchmarking

- Comparing company performance with competitors or industry standards.
- Example: A banking company evaluates their digital services by comparing them with those of major competitors.

✓ 3. Case Studies of Success and Failure

- Using historical data from successful or failed strategies as learning for future strategies.
- Example: A transportation company analyzes the success factors of Grab's expansion into various Southeast Asian countries.

✓ 4. Balanced Scorecard (BSC) Based Evaluation

- Using indicators from four BSC perspectives: **Financial, Customer, Internal Processes, and Learning and Growth** .
- Example: A pharmaceutical company evaluates their product innovation strategy by looking at its impact on customer satisfaction and market growth.

Conclusion

Strategy success evaluation is a crucial step in strategic management that allows companies to measure the effectiveness of their strategies, identify opportunities for improvement, and ensure adaptation to market changes. By using the right methods, companies can increase their competitiveness and ensure long-term growth.

Case Study: Strategy Evaluation in a Public Company

Background

PT XYZ is one of the largest public companies in Indonesia engaged in the manufacturing sector. In the last five years, the company has implemented a market expansion strategy by opening new factories in several areas. This strategy aims to increase production capacity, reduce logistics costs, and expand market reach.

However, after three years of implementation, the company faced several challenges such as increasing operational costs, changes in environmental regulations, and increasingly tight competition. A strategy evaluation was conducted to determine whether the expansion that had been carried out was in accordance with the initial objectives and whether strategic adjustments were needed.

Challenges Faced

1. **Increased Operating Costs**

- Production costs increased due to rising prices of raw materials and labor wages.
- Companies need to evaluate the efficiency of their supply chain and production processes.

1. **Regulatory Changes and Environmental Compliance**

- There is a new policy regarding emission standards that requires companies to invest in environmentally friendly technology.
- Additional costs for regulatory compliance need to be considered in the financial strategy.

1. **Increasing Competition**

- Competing companies began offering products with more competitive prices and superior technological innovation.
- Companies need to evaluate product differentiation strategies and added value for customers.

1. **Market Expansion Effectiveness**

- Has the expansion that has been carried out had a positive impact on revenue growth?
- Is the new factory location strategic in supporting distribution and supply chain?

Evaluation Methods Used

1. **Balanced Scorecard (BSC)**

- Using financial, customer, internal business process, and learning and growth perspectives to evaluate strategy.
- Example: Does investing in a new plant improve customer satisfaction and the company's competitiveness?

1. **ROI Analysis (Return on Investment)**

- Calculate the rate of return on factory expansion investment over a five-year period.

- Does the investment provide returns commensurate with the costs incurred?

1. **Benchmarking against Competitors**

- Comparing PT XYZ's expansion strategy with major competitors in the industry.
- Identifying the company's strengths and weaknesses compared to competitors in terms of price, quality and innovation.

1. **SWOT Analysis**

- Identify the strengths, weaknesses, opportunities and threats of the expansion strategy that has been implemented.
- Does this expansion strengthen the company's market position or does it increase business risks?

Evaluation Results

- **Profit:**
- The expansion managed to increase production by **30%** in three years.
- The company gained new market share in several previously underserved areas.
- **Weakness:**
- Operating costs increased by **15%** due to rising raw material and labor prices.
- Environmental regulations require additional investments that were not accounted for in the initial strategy.
- **Recommended Improvement Strategy:**
- Optimizing operational efficiency through **automation of production processes** .
- Implementing **product differentiation strategies** to increase added value

for customers.

- Establish partnerships with local suppliers to reduce logistics and raw material costs.
- Implementing **sustainability strategies** to meet environmental regulations and enhance corporate image.

Student Assignment

As a business strategy analyst, you are asked to evaluate the success of PT XYZ's expansion strategy and provide additional recommendations to improve the effectiveness of their strategy. Answer the following questions:

1. **Evaluation of Implementation Success**

- What factors contributed to the success of PT XYZ's expansion strategy?
- How can the strategies that have been implemented be improved to achieve more optimal results?

1. **Optimizing Operational Efficiency**

- What steps can companies take to reduce the impact of rising operating costs?
- How can companies use technology to improve production efficiency?

1. **Strategic Risk and Regulatory Analysis**

- How can companies ensure compliance with environmental regulations without sacrificing profitability?
- What strategies can be implemented to reduce risks in business expansion investments?

1. **Future Strategy Recommendations**

- If you were the Chief Strategy Officer (CSO) at PT XYZ, what strategies would you recommend to maintain the company's competitiveness?
- How can companies ensure continued growth with more flexible and adaptive strategies?

Expected Output:

- PT XYZ expansion strategy analysis report.
- Recommendations for improvement strategies to increase efficiency and competitiveness.
- A short presentation on strategic solutions for PT XYZ.

CHAPTER 13: Innovation and Strategic Management in the Era of Disruption

13.1 Paradigm Shift in Strategic Management

Understanding Paradigm Change in Strategic Management

The paradigm shift in strategic management refers to the shift in the way companies design, implement, and evaluate their strategies due to technological developments, changes in market behavior, and the dynamics of global competition.

According to **Christensen (2013)** , the digital era has changed the approach to business strategy from a traditional model based on stability and long-term planning to a more flexible, fast and innovation-based model.

Factors Driving Change in Strategy Paradigms

✔ 1. Digitalization and New Technologies

- Companies must adapt to technological advances such as **Artificial Intelligence (AI), Big Data, Cloud Computing, and the Internet of Things (IoT)**.

- Example: Amazon uses AI to improve customer experience through personalized product recommendations.

✓ 2. Changes in Consumer Behavior

- Consumers increasingly prioritize **convenience, speed and personalization** in services.
- Example: Netflix replaced the DVD rental industry with its subscription-based streaming service.

✓ 3. Increasing Competition and Globalization

- Companies are not only competing at the local level but also with more innovative and efficient global players.
- Example: Fintech startups like Gojek and OVO are changing the digital payments industry in Indonesia.

✓ 4. Business Model Changes

- The emergence of **business platforms, sharing economy, and subscription models** are replacing conventional business models.
- Example: Spotify and Apple Music shifted the way music is consumed from purchasing physical albums to a streaming model.

Strategies in Facing Paradigm Change

✓ 1. Digital Transformation

- Integrating technology into every aspect of business to increase efficiency and competitiveness.
- Example: Banks are adopting mobile banking to reduce dependence on physical services.

✓ 2. Continuous Innovation

- Companies must continue to innovate in products, services and operations to stay relevant.
- Example: Tesla is consistently developing electric and autonomous vehicle technology.

✓ 3. Data-Driven Business Strategy

- Using data as a basis for business decision making.
- Example: Google relies on data analytics to optimize its digital advertising.

✓ 4. Flexible and Adaptive Business Model

- Using an **Agile Strategy approach** to deal with rapid changes in the market.
- Example: A retail company adopts an omnichannel strategy to combine offline and online shopping experiences.

Conclusion

The paradigm shift in strategic management requires companies to be more flexible, innovative, and data-driven. By adopting technology-based strategies and more adaptive business models, companies can remain competitive in facing the challenges of the disruptive era.

13.2 Disruptive Innovation and Its Implications

Understanding Disruptive Innovation

Disruptive Innovation is an innovation that changes the way an industry works by replacing existing technologies or business models, often by offering simpler, cheaper, and more efficient solutions. The concept was first introduced by **Clayton Christensen (1997)** in his book *The Innovator's Dilemma* .

Disruptive Innovation often starts from previously underserved market segments before eventually dominating the main market and replacing incumbents.

Characteristics of Disruptive Innovation

✓ 1. Start from a Niche Market or Marginalized Segment

- Disruptive innovations often develop in markets that large companies do not consider profitable.
- Example: Netflix initially only provided a subscription-based DVD rental service before eventually disrupting the television and cinema industries with its streaming service.

✓ 2. Offers Cheaper and Easier to Use Solutions

- Innovative products or services are usually cheaper and more convenient to use than traditional alternatives.
- Example: Online transportation such as Gojek and Grab offer more efficient mobility solutions than conventional taxis.

✓ 3. Using New Technologies to Transform Business Models

- Disruptive Innovation typically relies on new technologies that enable large efficiencies and scale.
- Example: Airbnb uses digital technology to connect renters and property owners without the need to own physical assets.

✓ 4. Disrupt Existing Markets and Create New Standards

- Companies that adopt disruptive innovation often create new industry standards.
- Example: E-commerce such as Tokopedia and Shopee change consumer

shopping patterns from physical stores to online shopping.

Implications of Disruptive Innovation for Companies

✓ 1. Opportunities for New Companies (Startups & Innovators)

- Disruptive Innovation provides opportunities for new companies to enter industries previously dominated by incumbents.
- Example: Fintech such as OVO and Dana are changing the financial industry by providing digital payment services without the need for traditional banks.

✓ 2. Threats for Companies that Do Not Adapt

- Companies that fail to adapt to these changes may lose market share or even go out of business.
- Example: Kodak failed to adapt to digital camera technology and eventually lost its dominance in the photography industry.

✓ 3. Fundamental Changes in Business Models

- Companies must redesign their business strategies to be more flexible in facing market changes.
- Example: Traditional banks are now adopting digital banking services to compete with fintech.

✓ 4. Continuous Innovation as the Key to Survival

- Companies must continue to innovate to stay relevant and not be replaced by new competitors.
- Example: Apple continues to develop its product ecosystem with new

innovations to maintain customer loyalty.

Strategy for Facing Disruptive Innovation

✔ 1. Building a Culture of Innovation in the Company

- Encourage experimentation and development of new ideas to create more competitive products.

✔ 2. Invest in New Technologies

- Companies must be proactive in adopting technologies that support their business transformation.

✔ 3. Develop a Flexible Business Model

- Companies must be ready to adapt to market trends and change business strategies according to customer needs.

✔ 4. Collaboration with Startups or Acquisition of Technology Companies

- Large companies can partner with or acquire innovative startups to accelerate their digital transformation.

Conclusion

Disruptive Innovation has changed the business landscape across industries and requires companies to adapt quickly. Companies that are able to understand and respond to disruptive innovation with the right strategy will remain competitive and relevant in the long run.

13.3 Agile Strategy in Modern Management

Understanding Agile Strategy

Agile strategy is a flexible approach to business management that allows companies to respond quickly to change, adapt to dynamic environments, and develop innovative solutions in a short time. This method was first introduced in the software industry through **the Agile Manifesto (2001)** and has now been applied in various business sectors.

According to **Rigby, Sutherland, & Takeuchi (2016)** , Agile strategy emphasizes **speed, collaboration, experimentation, and continuous learning** to achieve competitive advantage.

Agile Strategy Principles

✓ **1. Continuous Iteration and Adaptation**

- Using an incremental approach to continuously improve business processes and results.
- Example: Spotify uses the Agile model to develop new features with an experimental approach based on user feedback.

✓ **2. Collaboration and Flexible Teams**

- Encourage cross-functional collaboration between teams within the organization to accelerate innovation.
- **squad and tribe**- based work system to increase productivity in product development.

✓ **3. Quick Response to Change**

- Adapting strategies based on market changes and customer needs.
- Example: Netflix continuously adjusts its recommendation algorithm

based on user behavior.

✅ 4. Focus on Customer Value

- Every business decision is oriented towards increasing value for customers.
- Example: Amazon implements an Agile strategy by optimizing customer experience through service innovations such as **One-Day Delivery and AI-driven Customer Support**.

✅ 5. Experimentation and Fast Learning

- Encourage trial and iteration to find the best solutions quickly.
- Example: Facebook applies the principle of **"Move Fast and Break Things"** in developing new features.

The Advantages of Agile Strategy in Modern Management

- **Increase the Speed of Innovation** → Enables companies to launch products faster than competitors.
- **Reducing the Risk of Big Mistakes** → Using an experiment-based approach to avoid large-scale failures.
- **Increased Responsiveness to Market** → Enables companies to quickly adjust strategies to changing market conditions.
- **Improve Team Collaboration** → Teams working in an Agile system have more effective and synergistic communication.

Challenges in Implementing Agile Strategy

- **Resistance to Change** → Not all organizations are ready to abandon traditional management approaches.
- **Resource Constraints** → Agile implementation requires investment in training and supporting technology.

- **Difficulty in Scalability** → Agile is easier to implement in small teams than in companies with complex hierarchies.

Conclusion

Agile strategy enables companies to be more flexible in facing changes, increase innovation, and provide added value to customers. By implementing Agile principles, organizations can respond more quickly to market dynamics and maintain their competitiveness in the era of disruption.

13.4 Case Study: Unicorn Companies and Their Innovation Strategies

Background

The tech and startup industry has seen rapid growth in the last decade, with the emergence of **unicorns** —startups valued at more than **$1 billion** . One unicorn that has successfully disrupted the Indonesian market is **Gojek** , which initially focused on app-based transportation services and has now developed into a digital ecosystem that includes payment, logistics, and e-commerce services.

Challenges Faced by Gojek

1. **Fierce Competition in the Technology Industry**

- The emergence of competitors such as Grab and Shopee which offer similar services with strategic differentiation.
- Companies must continue to innovate to maintain competitive advantage.

1. **Government Regulation**

- Changes in regulations related to online transportation and digital payments require Gojek to adapt quickly.

- Example: The Indonesian government has imposed a minimum fare rule for ride-hailing services.

1. **Sustainability of Business Models**

- Gojek must find a sustainable monetization strategy without relying on incentives and subsidies for users.
- Service diversification is a key strategy in maintaining business growth.

Gojek Innovation Strategy

✅ **1. Expansion into Multi-Sector Services (Super App Strategy)**

- Developing a digital ecosystem through the **Gojek Super App** , which combines transportation, food delivery, digital payments, and logistics services in one platform.
- **GoPay** services as a payment system connected to various merchants.

✅ **2. Strategic Alliances and Acquisitions**

- Investing and collaborating with other companies to expand its digital ecosystem.
- Example: Merger with Tokopedia to form **GoTo** , the largest digital ecosystem in Indonesia.

✅ **3. Utilization of Data and AI in Decision Making**

- Using **Big Data and Machine Learning** to improve operational efficiency and user experience.
- Example: AI algorithms for driver route optimization and food delivery time estimation.

✓ **4. Sustainability and ESG (Environmental, Social, and Governance) Strategy**

- Focusing on business sustainability by developing environmentally friendly and inclusive initiatives.
- **Gojek GoGreener** program which offers electric vehicle options for driver partners.

The Impact of Innovation on Gojek's Success

- **Increase customer loyalty** with integrated services in one application.
- **Assisting expansion into international markets** , such as Vietnam, Thailand, and the Philippines.
- **Increase valuation and global competitiveness** through merger with Tokopedia.
- **Improve operational efficiency** , reduce transaction costs, and optimize resource allocation.

Student Assignment

As a business strategy analyst, you are asked to evaluate the success of Gojek's innovation strategy and provide additional recommendations to improve their competitiveness. Answer the following questions:

1. **Evaluation of Gojek's Strategy Success**

- What factors contributed to the success of Gojek's innovation strategy?
- How will the merger with Tokopedia impact the growth of their digital ecosystem?

1. **Business Model Optimization**

- What additional steps can Gojek take to maintain their market position?

- How can Gojek increase profitability without relying on subsidies or user incentives?

1. **Market Risk and Regulation Analysis**

- How can Gojek adapt to changing government regulations in the technology industry?
- What strategies can be implemented to reduce risks in international expansion?

1. **Future Strategy Recommendations**

- If you were the Chief Strategy Officer (CSO) at Gojek, what innovation strategies would you recommend for long-term growth?
- How can companies further develop AI and Big Data technologies to improve their services?

Expected Output:

- Gojek innovation strategy analysis report.
- Recommended strategies to improve business competitiveness and sustainability.
- A short presentation on strategic solutions for Gojek.

CHAPTER 14: The Future of Strategic Management

14.1 Future Trends in Strategic Management

Understanding Future Trends in Strategic Management

Strategic management continues to evolve along with changes in the global business environment, technological advances, and sustainability demands. Companies must prepare for the future with more dynamic, data-driven, and sustainable strategies to stay relevant in the industry competition.

According to **Grant (2021)** , future trends in strategic management will not only focus on business growth, but also on the balance between profitability, social impact, and environmental sustainability.

Key Trends in Future Strategy Management

☑ 1. Digitalization and AI in Decision Making

- The application of **Artificial Intelligence (AI)** and **Big Data Analytics** is increasingly dominant in the strategic decision-making process.
- Example: Retail companies use AI to analyze customer behavior and optimize supply chains.

✓ 2. Focus on Sustainability and ESG (Environmental, Social, and Governance)

- Companies are increasingly required to consider sustainability aspects in their strategies.
- Example: Energy companies are starting to invest in renewable energy sources to reduce their carbon footprint.

✓ 3. Digital Transformation and Platform-Based Business Models

- Platform-based businesses and the sharing economy continue to grow.
- Example: Business models like Gojek and Airbnb allow individuals to participate in the digital economy with great flexibility.

✓ 4. Flexibility and Rapid Adaptation to Global Changes

- Companies must be more agile in responding to economic and geopolitical uncertainty.
- Example: The COVID-19 pandemic has pushed many companies to adopt hybrid work systems and more decentralized supply chains.

✓ 5. Increased Focus on Customer Experience (Customer-Centric Strategy)

- Companies that prioritize customer experience are more likely to experience higher loyalty and retention.
- Example: Apple and Tesla continue to develop unique user experiences through product and service innovation.

Impact of Future Trends on Strategy Management

- **Organizational Structure Changes** → Companies must be more flexible with more collaborative and technology-based work models.
- **Continuous Innovation** → Companies must continuously innovate their

products and services to remain competitive.

- **Use of Advanced Technology** → Blockchain, Internet of Things (IoT), and AI will increasingly play a role in business strategies.
- **Sustainability as a Global Standard** → Companies must integrate sustainability principles into all aspects of their business.

Conclusion

The future of strategic management will be dominated by digital technology, sustainability, and flexibility in facing market changes. Companies that are able to adopt these trends quickly will have a stronger competitive advantage in the global market.

14.2 The Role of Sustainability and ESG in Strategy

Understanding Sustainability and ESG in Business Strategy

Sustainability in business strategy refers to practices that ensure that companies can thrive in the long term while considering social, environmental, and governance impacts. ESG (**Environmental, Social, and Governance**) is a framework used to measure the sustainability and ethical impact of a company.

According to **Porter & Kramer (2011)** , companies that implement sustainability and ESG-based strategies can increase value for shareholders while contributing to society and the environment.

ESG Components in Strategy Management

✓ 1. Environmental (Environment)

- Focus on the company's efforts to reduce environmental impact and implement more environmentally friendly business.

- Example: A manufacturing company reduces carbon emissions and uses renewable energy for its operations.

✓ 2. Social (Social)

- Assess how the company interacts with employees, customers, suppliers, and the wider community.
- Examples: Employee wellness programs, human rights, and diversity and inclusion in the workforce.

✓ 3. Governance (Corporate Governance)

- Reflects how the company is managed with the principles of transparency, accountability and compliance with regulations.
- Examples: Ethical board of directors structure, anti-corruption practices, and protection of shareholder rights.

Benefits of Implementing ESG in Business Strategy

✓ 1. Improve Company Reputation

- Companies that implement ESG principles are more trusted by customers, investors and business partners.

✓ 2. Reducing Regulatory and Legal Risks

- Compliance with environmental and social standards helps companies avoid fines and legal sanctions.

✓ 3. Improve Operational Efficiency

- More sustainable use of resources can reduce long-term operating costs.

✓ 4. Better Access to Capital and Investment

- Investors are increasingly taking ESG performance into account before investing in a company.

✓ 5. Increase Customer and Employee Loyalty

- Consumers tend to choose brands that care about sustainability, and employees are more motivated to work for companies that have a clear social vision.

Challenges in Implementing ESG in Strategy

- **High Initial Costs** → Implementing environmentally friendly technologies and social programs requires large initial investments.
- **Lack of Consistent Standards** → Not all countries have uniform ESG standards, posing challenges for multinational companies.
- **The Need for Data Transparency** → Companies must provide clear and accountable sustainability reports.
- **Difficulty Measuring ESG Impact** → Some aspects of ESG are difficult to measure quantitatively, such as social and cultural impacts.

Conclusion

Integrating sustainability and ESG into business strategy is not just a trend, but a new standard in corporate operations. By implementing ESG, companies can increase competitiveness, build a better reputation, and create long-term value for all stakeholders.

14.3 Adaptation Strategies to Global Change

Understanding Adaptation Strategies to Global Change

Adaptation strategy to global change is an approach taken by companies to adjust to the dynamics of the economy, society, politics, and technology that continue to develop at the global level. Companies that are able to anticipate and respond to global change quickly will have higher competitiveness.

According to **Kotler & Keller (2021)** , a successful organization is an organization that is able to adapt to global trends and create flexible strategies in the face of market uncertainty.

Factors Driving Global Change

✓ **1. Globalization and Digitalization**

- Companies must adapt to digital technologies and globalization that accelerate changes in markets and industries.
- Example: Retail companies are now integrating omnichannel strategies with e-commerce to reach a wider market.

✓ **2. Climate Change and Sustainability Issues**

- Companies need to adapt their operations to increasingly stringent environmental regulations.
- Example: Automotive companies like Tesla are turning to electric vehicles to reduce carbon emissions.

✓ **3. Economic and Geopolitical Uncertainty**

- Global economic crises, trade wars and political instability can impact companies' supply chains and investment strategies.
- Example: Multinational companies develop market diversification strate-

gies to reduce dependence on one country.

✅ 4. Changes in Demographics and Consumer Behavior

- Companies must understand population trends, such as the growth of the more digitally savvy millennial and Gen Z generations.
- Example: The banking industry is turning to digital banking services to meet the needs of the younger generation who prefer online transactions.

Adaptation Strategies in Facing Global Change

✅ 1. Flexibility in Business Model

- Companies must adopt business models that can adapt to market changes.
- Example: Netflix changed its business model from DVD rentals to a global streaming service.

✅ 2. Digital Transformation and Technological Innovation

- Adopting technologies such as AI, IoT, and blockchain to increase efficiency and competitiveness.
- Example: Logistics companies use AI to improve supply chain efficiency and delivery of goods.

✅ 3. Strengthening Sustainability in Business Strategy

- Implementing ESG policies to reduce regulatory risks and increase attractiveness to investors and customers.
- Example: Cosmetic companies are turning to organic ingredients and eco-friendly packaging to appeal to environmentally conscious consumers.

✅ 4. Market and Supply Chain Diversification

- Reduce risk by reaching multiple markets and not relying on one country or region.
- Example: Electronics companies like Samsung manufacture goods in different countries to avoid supply chain disruptions.

✓ 5. Improving Human Resources (HR) Capabilities

- Train employees to have skills that are relevant to global industrial developments.
- Example: Technology companies provide training related to cloud computing and artificial intelligence to increase the competitiveness of their workforce.

Positive Impacts of Adaptation to Global Change

- **Enhancing competitiveness and long-term growth**
- **Reducing business risks due to economic and geopolitical uncertainty**
- **Strengthening business continuity and compliance with international regulations**
- **Increase customer loyalty with strategies that are in line with global trends**

Conclusion

Adapting to global change is a critical element of modern business strategy. Companies that are able to understand global trends, implement innovation, and maintain flexibility in their strategies will be better prepared to face challenges and capitalize on opportunities in an ever-evolving market.

14.4 Case Study: Implementation of Sustainability Strategy in Indonesian Companies

Background

Companies in Indonesia are increasingly recognizing the importance of sustainability in their business operations. With increasing pressure from regulators, investors, and consumers, many companies are starting to adopt sustainability strategies that focus on **environmental, social, and governance (ESG) aspects** . One company that has successfully implemented a sustainability strategy is **PT Unilever Indonesia Tbk** .

As part of the global Unilever, PT Unilever Indonesia has taken concrete steps to integrate sustainability into its business strategy. The company is committed to environmentally friendly initiatives, social responsibility, and transparent governance to improve its competitiveness in the long term.

Challenges Faced by PT Unilever Indonesia

1. **Waste Reduction and Carbon Emissions**

- Increasing environmental regulations require companies to reduce the environmental impact of their business operations.
- PT Unilever Indonesia must innovate in the production process to be more efficient and environmentally friendly.

1. **Sustainable Resources**

- Companies must ensure that the raw materials used come from sustainable sources.
- Example: Use of certified palm oil to reduce the impact of deforestation.

1. **Increasing Consumer Awareness of Environmentally Friendly Products**

- Consumers are increasingly concerned about sustainability and tend to choose products that have a positive social and environmental impact.
- Companies must communicate their sustainability values to consumers effectively.

1. **Transparency and Accountability in ESG**

- PT Unilever Indonesia needs to ensure that they comply with ESG standards and report their sustainability performance transparently.

Implemented Sustainability Strategies

✔ 1. Environmentally Friendly Production

- Using energy efficiency technology in the production process.
- Reduce plastic use with recyclable packaging.

✔ 2. Social Initiatives and Community Empowerment

- Health and sanitation education programs for the community through cleanliness campaigns.
- Empowering micro and small businesses through partnership programs with local shops.

✔ 3. Sustainable Supply Chain Management

- Work with suppliers who have sustainability commitments.
- Implementing sustainability policies in the selection of raw materials.

✔ 4. Transparency and ESG Reporting

- Publish sustainability reports that adhere to global standards such as **the Global Reporting Initiative (GRI)** .
- Involving stakeholders in the evaluation of the company's social and environmental impacts.

Positive Impacts of Sustainability Strategies

- **Increased consumer loyalty** that is more concerned about environmental issues.
- **Operational cost efficiency** by reducing waste and increasing energy efficiency.
- **The attraction for investors** is that companies with good ESG performance tend to be more stable and profitable in the long term.
- **Compliance with** increasingly stringent environmental and social regulations.

Student Assignment

As a business strategy analyst, you are asked to evaluate the implementation of sustainability strategy in PT Unilever Indonesia and provide additional recommendations to improve its effectiveness. Answer the following questions:

1. **Evaluation of Sustainability Strategy Success**

- What factors contribute to the success of PT Unilever Indonesia's sustainability strategy?
- How can companies increase the positive impact of their sustainability initiatives?

1. **Sustainable Business Model Optimization**

- What additional steps can companies take to accelerate the implementation of sustainability strategies?

- How can sustainability strategies be linked to product and service innovation?

1. **ESG Risk and Regulation Analysis**

- How can PT Unilever Indonesia ensure compliance with evolving environmental regulations?
- What strategies can be implemented to reduce ESG risks that may impact a company's reputation?

1. **Future Strategy Recommendations**

- If you were the Chief Sustainability Officer (CSO) at PT Unilever Indonesia, what sustainability initiatives would you propose to improve the company's competitiveness?
- How can companies better integrate ESG principles throughout their supply chain and business operations?

Expected Output:

- PT Unilever Indonesia sustainability strategy analysis report.
- Additional strategy recommendations to improve sustainability effectiveness.
- A short presentation on strategic solutions for PT Unilever Indonesia.

206

About Author

D r. Ali Kesuma, born in on February 1963, son of Wijaya Kesuma (late) and Netty Tan (late). Bachelor of Accounting (1987), Master of Management with a concentration in Finance (1996) and Doctor of Economics with a concentration in Marketing Management (2004), is currently a permanent lecturer in the undergraduate Management study program at UNDA University with the academic position of Senior Lecturer.

In 1990 he was selected as Exemplary Lecturer I of Kopertis Region XI Kalimantan, served as Chancellor of UNDA University until 2022. Author of several research articles published in several accredited national journals, and wrote several book manuscripts that are currently in the queue for publication at publishers, such as the books Marketing 5.0, Human Resource Management, Strategic Management etc.

Communication: E-mail: Alikesuma@unda.ac.id

Bibliography

Ansoff, H. I. (1965). *Corporate Strategy: An Analytic Approach to Business Policy for Growth and Expansion.* McGraw-Hill.

Barney, J. (1991). *Firm Resources and Sustained Competitive Advantage.* Journal of Management.

Chandler, A. D. (1962). *Strategy and Structure: Chapters in the History of the Industrial Enterprise.* MIT Press.

David, F. R. (2020). *Strategic Management: A Competitive Advantage Approach, Concepts and Cases.* Pearson.

Kaplan, R. S., & Norton, D. P. (1996). *The Balanced Scorecard: Translating Strategy into Action.* Harvard Business Press.

Kim, W. C., & Mauborgne, R. (2005). *Blue Ocean Strategy: How to Create Uncontested Market Space and Make the Competition Irrelevant.* Harvard Business Review Press.

Pella, D. A. (2021). *Strategic Management: From Analysis to Implementation.* Jakarta: PT Gramedia.

Porter, M. E. (1980). *Competitive Strategy: Techniques for Analyzing Industries and Competitors.* Free Press.

Prahalad, C. K., & Hamel, G. (1990). *The Core Competence of the Corporation.* Harvard Business Review.

Ramli, Y., & Kartini, D. (2022). *Manajemen Strategi: Teori dan Praktik.* Bandung: Penerbit ITB.

Rivai, A., & Prawironegoro, D. (2019). *Manajemen Strategi: Konsep, Kasus, dan Implementasi.* Jakarta: Mitra Wacana Media.

Weihrich, H. (1982). *The TOWS Matrix—A Tool for Situational Analysis.* Long

Range Planning.